WE ARE HERE

The Voice of
The New Perspective

Ron and Denny Reynolds

Trafford
PUBLISHING

Note for Librarians: A cataloguing record for this book is available from Library and Archives Canada at www.collectionscanada.ca/amicus/index-e.html
ISBN 978-1-4251-1554-8

Printed in Victoria, BC, Canada. Printed on paper with minimum 30% recycled fibre. Trafford's print shop runs on "green energy" from solar, wind and other environmentally-friendly power sources.

Offices in Canada, USA, Ireland and UK

Book sales for North America and international:
Trafford Publishing, 6E–2333 Government St.,
Victoria, BC V8T 4P4 CANADA
phone 250 383 6864 (toll-free 1 888 232 4444)
fax 250 383 6804; email to orders@trafford.com
Book sales in Europe:
Trafford Publishing (UK) Limited, 9 Park End Street, 2nd Floor
Oxford, UK OX1 1HH UNITED KINGDOM
phone +44 (0)1865 722 113 (local rate 0845 230 9601)
facsimile +44 (0)1865 722 868; info.uk@trafford.com
Order online at:
trafford.com/07-0012

10 9 8 7 6 5 4

Contents

I

Introduction

By Ron

This is a story of spiritual awakening. It occurred at the turn of the millennium, between 1987 and 2004. I will be as objective as I can in telling my story, at the same time realizing that some of you will have difficulty with it because it cannot be validated in scientific terms. No one feels this dilemma more than I do because I spent fifty years in radio broadcasting, an industry that seldom acknowledges the kind of experience I had.

I had begun a dialogue with a consciousness that was not physical. I had discovered a way to tap into a source of deep wisdom. At the same time that this phenomenon was occurring, I was the evening news anchor at KCBS radio, the All News Station in San Francisco. It was my responsibility to always be objective and maintain fairness and honesty in reporting the events of the day. If it became known I was having these strange experiences away from work, my professional status might be challenged. Therefore, I was

1

reluctant to share them. Now, I want to be totally open as I come out of the spiritual closet to tell you my story. None of this book is fictionalized. It is a chronicle of real experiences.

What I experienced happened on a level of perception beyond the material world of seeing, hearing, smelling, tasting, and touching. My experience cannot be objectively measured, but from my perspective there is no denying its validity. What I am reporting is personal, and therefore subjective. It all took place in my mind and could be appreciated by others only after I shared out loud the message I was receiving.

What would people think, I worried, if they knew a respected voice of authority who reports the news every day was having such unusual experiences? How could I explain that I was connecting with an "inner voice?" I knew this was not the same phenomenon experienced by psychiatric patients when they report hearing voices commanding and controlling them. My voice was gentle and loving, never intrusive, and appeared only when invited by me. This was a spiritual experience in the tradition of Edgar Cayce, an American healer known as "the sleeping prophet;" Neale Donald Walsch, the chronicler of *Conversations with God*; Helen Schucman, who was responsible for taking the dictation that became *A Course in Miracles*; Jane Roberts, who produced all the Seth material; and countless others.

This was not a new experience for me. As a 13-year-old boy I became interested in ventriloquism, bought books on the subject and learned how to throw my voice. My grandmother bought me a dummy and he and I became local celebrities. What's particularly interesting about this phase of my life is the fact that I was often as surprised by what came out of the dummy's mouth as the audience was. While performing as a child ventriloquist I now believe I was beginning to access my "inner voice." Therefore, it comes as no surprise that the channeling experience described in this book unfolded in my life. What I know from this experience is if it could happen to me...it can happen to you. And it will, upon your invitation.

Perhaps you have feelings that it already has happened to you. Have you ever been so involved in a creative project that you lose yourself and time seems to disappear? Have you had inspired thoughts in desperate times that you feel were heaven sent? Have you ever felt someone was watching over and guiding you, like a guardian angel? Have you ever ignored your inner wisdom only to find yourself in a mess as a result of your failure to listen? Have you had times when you've said to yourself, "Gee, I knew that?"

These were times when you were in touch with your Inner Voice. To some it isn't a voice; it's a feeling, an intuitive knowing. The point is you have the ability to recognize and utilize this God-given gift. You can choose to put this part of yourself in charge of your life. You can use your experience with this energy to enhance every aspect of your being. You can know you are never alone. To experience your Inner Voice you must ask It to come forth. Spirit speaks by invitation.

All of the dialogue in this book actually took place and was tape-recorded as it occurred. As the conversations were recorded the words were coming from me...or rather through me. I was not consciously thinking, or forming senten-ces—much like my extemporaneous teenage ventriloquism experience. What I did was enter an altered state of consciousness, a meditative state in which my "thinking mind" was quieted, and then I was asked questions. I observed words as they passed through my awareness. I then repeated the words out loud one by one into the tape recorder, in such a manner that I usually wasn't sure of what was being said. By the end of a sentence my conscious mind had often lost track of the beginning of the sentence. For this reason, during the early channeling sessions, I often struggled with the words. Whenever I engaged in this kind of resistance I would gently be admonished by the source of the information to relax and stop interfering with the process.

Supporters of this phenomenon call the process channeling. Skeptics enjoy calling it imaginary thinking. To those who say to me, "It was just your imagination," I say, yes. My ears were not hearing the voice. My mind was hearing the voice. I became the reporter, repeating out loud the words that were passing through my imagination. I have come firmly to believe that our imagination is our sixth sense. I think we experience life not only through sight, sound, taste, smell, and touch, but also through the rich world of imagination—that creative playground of the mind. Science would have you believe that all of life's experience is chemical activity occurring in that "wet piece of meat" we call the brain. The question science fails to address is where does inspiration originate? When we are inspired—when we create—where does that inspiration come from that floats through our imagination and then comes into the world in the form of great paintings, inspired music, innovative inventions, and memorable literature?

Before my wife and I were able to understand the source of the channeled information in a way that satisfied our curiosity, we simply referred to the mysterious source as "The We." That's because every session began with the greeting, "We are here." In time we began to recognize "The We" as not only a dear and loving friend but also our wisest advisor and teacher.

Denny and I have written and published two other books, *The New Perspective: Ten Tools for Self-Transformation* and *Art of Relationship: The New Perspective*. This is our third book in *The New Perspective Trilogy* and it chronicles the events that unfolded over a span of three decades. The information we received became the inspiration for the first two books.

Throughout this book I am your narrator. My wife Denny is the interviewer, presiding over and directing the question and answer sessions. Her words are clearly identified throughout this work. I've chosen to label the responses spoken by "The We" with the designation HS. This allows you, the reader, to attribute the information to whatever source bests fits your belief system. Some may prefer to think of HS as being the Human Subconscious, that part of the mind below the conscious level that holds information we've heard or read, but do not consciously remember. This is known as cryptomnesia, or hidden memories that can be accessed through hypnosis, meditation, or other altered states. Others may prefer to have HS stand for Higher Self. Many people believe we each have a higher, wiser aspect of ourselves that can be accessed once the ego mind has been quieted, once we are able, as the Bible says, to "be still and know." A third explanation may be that HS is Holy Spirit. Consider the possibility that I connected, and you also can connect, with what *A Course in Miracles* calls the teacher within all of us, the Voice for God. *A Course in Miracles* (on page 75 of the *Manual for Teachers*) says, "Consciousness is the receptive mechanism, receiving messages from above or below; from the Holy Spirit or the ego." The *Course* also says (on page 85 of the *Manual for Teachers*), "The Holy Spirit is described as the remaining communication link between God and His separated Sons...the Holy Spirit abides in the part of your mind that is part of the Christ Mind. He represents your Self and your Creator, Who are one. He speaks for God and also for you, being joined with both."

I'll leave it up to you to decide the source of the information that came through me.

Ron Reynolds

Introduction

By Denny

Even though I was with Ron the day he had his first experience with the consciousness we've come to call "The We," I found it very difficult to believe that he wasn't just making up this unusual event. Ron claimed he was tapping into a consciousness that felt separate from his own. He asked me if I would be willing to ask this consciousness questions while he entered a light trance. I became intrigued by this idea and agreed to participate in this experiment. I found it challenging to ask questions in a way that would make sense. At this point I didn't know if I was talking to Ron or Ron's Higher Self or something beyond that. We were both so curious that the first questions I asked of "The We" were "who are you" and "where do you come from?" I was greatly intrigued by their response; "We exist on a level that connects us to all human beings. We express in slightly different forms with each connection we make, for we call upon inherent abilities and information in each individual channel. Therefore, we may seem to be different voices, but we are the One Voice of Spirit."

As our familiarity with the energy of this consciousness grew, we found ourselves using "The We" as consultants for making life choices as well as a sounding board for our Spiritual quest. As Ron and I read the transcripts from our question and answer sessions it became quite clear to me that this consciousness was very different from Ron's.

The ideas that came forth from "The We" challenged our beliefs and expanded our perspective. I was humbled to be in the presence of an energy that could bring forth such profound information. For me, the challenge of engaging "The We" in these dialogues was to get my ego-self out of the way and to allow whatever was about to happen. As I struggled to ask the right questions I became aware that if I just relaxed and tuned inward, the question that needed to be asked would come forth from some deeply inspired source within me.

I believe that many of the questions I asked were inspired by my own personal link to HS. "The We" have said many times that we each have our own unique connection to their energy and all we need to do is call on them and they will show up to guide, advise, and inform.

Writing spiritual books and teaching the principle that all our physical experiences are created from our inner reality has become a passion for Ron and me. Early on we were told by "The We," "If you do nothing else during the remainder of your lives but help teach that basic concept and exemplify it in your lives and keep coming back to that perspective—that view of reality—you will have done your work. There is no other purpose in physical existence than to recognize who is the wizard behind the curtain."

When Ron first had this experience we saw that if he could do it, I could do it and anyone who wanted could do it. We have learned that all you need to do to have this experience is to ask. As "The We" says: "Spirit speaks by invitation."

Denny Reynolds

II

Introducing the We

A Few of Our Favorite Things

Here are some of the early messages that not only got our attention, but kindled our determination to find out all we possibly could about this mysterious voice we had nicknamed "The We."

We are here to remind you...
—All problems are messengers. They bring forth a signal that says here is where faith is missing. When faith is restored, problems solve themselves, as they have no further need to exist.
—No good purpose is served by judging people harshly for the behavior or actions that come from their lack of awareness. There are two states: consciousness and unconsciousness. Bring only light to darkness.
—Allow vision to replace sight. Sight sees only the body. Vision recognizes the Christ within.
—Contentment comes from being one with the content

of your mind. To be discontent is to be out of accord with the content of your mind. Peace and contentment come from recognizing the unity of all that is. Disharmony and discontent result from believing that anything or anyone is separate from you.

We Are Here

The year was 1987. My thirty-three year career in broadcasting had taken an abrupt turn. After twelve years with KNBR, a popular music station in San Francisco, I was out of work. Broadcasting had been my life since 1954. I was thirteen years old when I became a disc jockey. Radio had consumed me ever since. Now, suddenly unemployed, I wasn't sure what I should do, let alone what I wanted to do. But I knew time would have to pass before I could even look for another job.

During the next several months I read dozens of spiritual and self-help books and explored a number of philosophies, both perennial and new age. One of my most meaningful growth experiences came when I encountered a process called Holotropic Breathwork® developed by Dr. Stanislav Grof. That's when I first heard from "The We."

I was perhaps fifteen to twenty minutes into the mind-expanding journey of rhythmic breathing, accompanied by evocative music, when my body did a very strange thing. It seemed to take control and breathe me. I was no longer deliberately breathing in and out to the rhythm of the music. A part of me seemed to have taken flight. It was as if I was no longer confined to my body. I remember passing through a number of swirling blobs of energy, all filled with incredibly beautiful colors. There were shades of red, orange, yellow, and blue, blending eventually into magenta and violet. As the journey continued I began to feel free and light, liberated, weightless; no longer confined to the boundaries of my body.

Suddenly a voice in my mind spoke, saying: "We are here. We are here to accompany you on your journey of Self-discovery. We will answer all your questions, tell you anything you want to know, take you anywhere you wish to go. We are here and we will remain with you on this journey."

What followed was a timeless interval of profound personal revelation. I later learned from my wife Denny, who was acting as my sitter—keeping me physically safe during the Holotropic Breathwork® session, that the journey had taken more than three hours. During that time the voice lovingly answered all of my questions as soon as I thought them. When I had questions regarding past lives I was shown scenes that were significant to issues I'm working on in this life. When I wondered about specific experiences in this life that I didn't understand I was given answers that provided some of the most helpful insights I had ever received about who I am. This new information shed light on significant events that I had not previously understood. For the first time, every aspect of my life was beginning to make sense. I was suddenly able to embrace parts of myself that I had been ashamed of. I was given a treasured gift. I received insights that provided a larger perspective that allowed me, for the first time, to begin to love many of the previously unloved aspects of myself.

I wasn't sure what to make of this unusual experience.

It had happened in my mind, in my imagination, but it did not feel like it was imagined or made up. It felt like I was having a conversation, a relationship with someone or something outside of myself—a voiceless voice. After I asked each of my questions, I did not consciously form in my mind the answer that followed. From my perspective it was very clear which part of the conversation was coming from me. Words and sentences that did not feel like my own were coming from somewhere else. In my mind I formed the questions and much to my amazement and fascination the answers were provided.

In reading about Holotropic Breathwork® I have learned that breathers often report experiences of a transpersonal nature, enjoying a blissful, expanded state of consciousness, going beyond ordinary states of reality. It was not until several years after Holotropic Breathwork® that it occurred to me that the voice coming through me might have been a channeling. I define channeling as the ability to become the vehicle through which information flows from a source outside of the ego self. I think that is what I experienced and I believe everyone is capable of doing so as well.

I'm not sure what I expected during my first attempt at channeling, but what a pleasant surprise it was to be greeted by the familiar words, "We are here."

Over time I have developed a very specific ritual that I now use to initiate the channeling experience. This ritual helps me induce the trance that allows me to enter an altered state of consciousness. So far the process has never failed me.

If you wish to have a channeling experience you may

find my ritual helpful, or you might prefer to develop your own technique. Here's my process: First, I enter into a state of deep relaxation, slowly focusing my attention on each part of my body until it begins to tingle with what I call "conscious awareness." Then, I clear my mind and quiet the chatter of the ego-mind by taking a number of deep breaths. I then recite a mantra that I learned years ago which helps me remember my true Spiritual nature and my connection to Divine Source.

I am the Soul.

I am the Light Divine

I am Love

I am will

I am fixed design.

This helps me remember that I am more than my body and that my mind is capable of receiving messages from above as well as below, as *A Course in Miracles* says: "...from Holy Spirit or the ego." Whichever voice I choose to invite will prevail.

Issuing an invitation to Spirit is the next order of business. I issue that invitation and state my intention by saying, "I invite Spirit to speak through me for my higher good and the higher good of all concerned."

When I channel, my experience is quite dreamlike. At the end of the session, when I come out of the light trance, my recollection of the experience fades quickly—much as dreams do upon awakening. For this reason I have a tape recorder available for each session to capture word for word exactly what comes through, rather than trusting my memory. It was only after I had played back the tapes and transcribed the material that I began to truly appreciate the value of the channeled information as I read the transcripts.

The conversations were initially very private, involving just my wife Denny and me. We are two people with both feet firmly planted on the ground and were originally not at all eager to go public with this experience. After all, I was earning my living as an objective radio newsman and Denny was a psychotherapist, licensed by the state of California and practicing since 1986. Eventually, as we became more comfortable with the phenomenon, the audience for the channeling sessions grew to include close friends and over time anyone who felt called to participate. You will become acquainted with some of these friends and associates as you read along. In some instances, we use real names, with the individuals' permission. In other cases we identify people only as "Male," or "Female" questioners.

We have learned from "The We" that channeling is something that can be done by anyone and everyone. They say the Voice of Spirit speaks to or through all who invite It. We were also told that it's helpful to have a second person, other than the channel, asking the questions. Once the channel enters the altered state it becomes difficult, if not counter productive, to have to engage the conscious mind in order to think of and ask questions. With someone else assuming this "thinking task," the channel can remain in a mentally passive state, allowing Spirit to flow through the channel unimpeded by the egoic "thinking mind."

Who Are the We?

From the very beginning Denny and I were quizzing the voice hoping to learn more about the source of the information that was coming through. We liked the message and we were most curious about the messenger. Clearly my voice was speaking the words, but it didn't feel like my mind was formulating the thoughts or creating the answers to Denny's questions. The responses and concepts were often information that was quite foreign to both of us.

The first description we received regarding the source of the information was somewhat vague. The voice presented itself as a plurality, "The We." They described themselves as information sorters who, when called upon, find truth and wisdom applicable to the situation at hand. They reminded us that the information is never anything we don't already know, but they pointed out that our "focus is often elsewhere and for that reason we are momentarily distracted from the truth—the truth that could set you free."

Here is what we learned:

HS: Perhaps it would be appropriate at this time to explain that we come from another dimension that has consciousness based in a non-physical realm of existence. Our skill is being able to help you access information that may not be readily apparent to you as you function within the intricate and complicated stories of your own creation. So our purpose is to help you maneuver through the illusion and to assist you in recognizing the significance of the relationship or situation in which you find yourself.

DENNY: The energy of "The We"...I'm trying to understand if you are on the causal plane, or if you are a gathering of fragments, or if your energy is different from that?

HS: The very concept of a causal plane is foreign to us. It is a descriptive term that has come from the mind of man...from imagination. It is valid for them within their universe, but within our frame of reference it has no significance beyond its existence as an idea. Our frame of reference is that we originate in pure consciousness and have no physical manifestation nor any need to have physical manifestation in order to do our work. We have joyous and blissful forms of self-expression and satisfaction. We play in the area of the interconnections between individuals, in that we can play in an unlimited arena of consciousness, information and experiences.

DENNY: What is your connection to the channel?

HS: We are an aspect of his consciousness ignited by the moment in which he instigated connection by inviting our presence. We are connected to many other such beings and have many, many, many avenues of expression.

DENNY: So when I hear my voice of intuition, am I tapping into the same source?

HS: You are experiencing us in a slightly different manner. Each connection is different and the result of each connection is different.

DENNY: The channel has asked me to ask you where he and I are in this process, and where we are going in relationship to "The We." What needs to be done to facilitate this situation?

HS: We would suggest that everything is "on course" in

this interaction, as is the case with every other aspect of every individual's life. There are no right and wrong ways to do things. From moment to moment, as different thoughts pass through the channel's mind, he will make different choices that will color this channeling experience. Any experience in life is altered and rearranged from thought to thought. This is an opportunity to view once again examples of how the experiences that seem to come to you in life are, in reality, coming from you and are created from your vast unlimited inner universe. So the successes and failures, that the channel has judged and labeled as the process unfolds, will be symbolic of the channel's growth in facilitating these experiences.

He will have to deal with his doubts in the area of channeling as much as his doubts in all other areas of his life. The same principles apply here as apply in any other undertaking. Your experience will vary moment to moment, based on your belief as to what is possible, or your belief about how things work, or what is true and what is not.

DENNY: I'd like to talk about my work for a moment. The area of psychotherapy is so limiting in its concepts. I find much more excitement in the other books I'm reading that provide larger pictures of who and what we are.

HS: Psychology has developed a well-organized field of information, but its "scientific nature" has filled it with limitations, allowing only certain concepts to be accepted, while automatically rejecting so many other possibilities.

DENNY: I keep searching for a larger framework to be able to communicate with higher aspects of consciousness to enable each individual to see himself in an expanded way.

HS: We would suggest that the basic work is as follows:

It is helpful for people to grasp the concept that they are more than their body. They are Spirit, come here in physicality for a series of experiences. The experiences are all created from an inner reality...the inner universe that is the real you. From that inner Self come all the symbols that you can then interact with and relate to, to learn and grow.

Once this information is truly accepted by the being, the transformation has occurred and the being can see it no other way when making an honest assessment of reality. They may tend to forget the experience; but if in your work you continually bring them back to that concept it will help them moment-by-moment, case-by-case, problem-by-problem, challenge-by-challenge, or opportunity-by-opportunity.

DENNY: And then explore what the symbol represents?

HS: We would suggest that if you do nothing else during the remainder of your lives but help teach that basic concept and exemplify it in your lives and keep coming back to that perspective, that view of reality, you will have done your work. And they will have done their work. There is no other purpose in physical existence than to recognize who is "the wizard behind the curtain."

You are a spark of the Divine and everything that materializes as physical symbols is part of the Divine. And so, none of your life experience or existence is in spite of you, it is because of you. The Divine You creates all things.

DENNY: I have sometimes felt during sessions as a therapist that I have been in touch with you while working with some of my clients. It felt like, as I got out of my own way, incredible stuff came through me from a source beyond me.

HS: You did successfully accomplish that. We exist on a level that connects us to all human beings. We express in slightly different forms with each connection we make, for we call upon inherent abilities and information in each individual channel. Therefore, we may seem to be different voices, but we are the One Voice of Spirit.

DENNY: So when my client got in touch with her own voice within, are you saying that you were speaking to or through her?

HS: That is correct.

DENNY: And my facilitating was helping her to open enough to hear from you and get in touch with the larger picture?

HS: Yes, and helping yourself simultaneously.

DENNY: I have another question. In my psychotherapy work yesterday with a client, I felt a shift. Things felt different. I felt like I was inviting you to be a guiding part of the therapy.

HS: It would be helpful to understand that we were there. We are everywhere. As we have said before, we speak with many voices, through those individuals who invite our presence.

It might help you to understand that a desire to know certain information is in itself an invitation for us to participate. Ours is a consciousness that is skilled in organizing and retrieving information.

DENNY: If we had a desire to know about past events that led to the taking in of certain negative beliefs, could we call on you to help retrieve that information?

HS: We prefer not to get lost in the specifics of any given soul's story. We can be helpful in contributing information that helps a person align with his true nature, rather than being caught in his story. We can provide an opportunity to reframe, to shift perspective, to see below the surface of what appears to be.

Again remember, all of your physical reality is symbolic of energy, beliefs, systems that exist in an inner, non-physical realm.

DENNY: Okay. Yesterday I did the first part of an EMDR session with a client. (EMDR is Eye Movement Desensitization and Reprocessing, a therapeutic healing technique especially helpful in relieving Post Traumatic Stress Disorder.) The client was focused on her story. When that was completed, I experienced an opening where I felt like you were participating in the session in assisting the client to the larger picture.

HS: We participate by assisting the consciousness of the individual in an awareness of the significance of a thought in a given moment.

DENNY: Hmm, I'm not totally understanding, but I will continue to play with the concept.

HS: We will be more specific. In the process of the eye movement, a mechanical condition occurs that alters the consciousness of the person moving the eyes. It is a tool, much like a drug is a tool to alter consciousness. The moving of the eyes alters physical mechanisms to a degree that pertinent ideas enter the consciousness. In this altered or expanded state of consciousness insights from the highest level of one's being become available. You are able to look past the stories you tell yourself to see a basic truth.

We help bring forth that truth, that wisdom which goes beyond your stories.

DENNY: Well, yesterday I really felt an altered consciousness with everyone I worked with, more deeply altered than anything I've previously experienced.

HS: Let us remind you of something spoken of here on another occasion. Your physical sensations during states of altered consciousness are reminders or symbols that let you know that Spirit is flowing in your life.

DENNY: Yes, that's what I was very aware of. I was just trying to figure out the connection between that and your consciousness.

HS: The connection is that *all energy* is interconnected. Our relationship to you is that we are absolutely connected to each other in a non-physical manner. We are a part of you, of humanity, in your many forms on this planet.

Perhaps it would be of assistance if we describe our existence. Our nature is consciousness in non-physical form. We are much like the person operating the holographic device in your Star Trek presentation. We enjoy a perspective that allows us to view all of the physical events and properties of your reality in the same manner as the Star Trek character does when visiting the holodeck.

Our consciousness can function with much less limitation, allowing us to do the extensive work we are called upon to do. You also have experienced this state of non-physicality, but at the present moment you have chosen to limit your abilities (in order) to gain the experience of physicality.

DENNY: I understand, and I remember years ago seeing a movie about a computer game. The characters within the game had a consciousness of their own, unique from that being who was playing the game.

HS: But interconnected. And in that same way we are interconnected with you and with all the other characters in your hologram.

DENNY: And all the other characters in every other hologram?

HS: That is correct.

DENNY: Hmmm, for the last several days that is the idea of reality that has been formulating in me. I feel like I'm beginning to get the bigger picture.

☙☙

On another channeling occasion in March of 1998 we were curious to know more about this unique voice that we were calling "The We." Perhaps this was another example of our common human need to label, define, and put things into categories.

DENNY: As far as you guys, "The We," are concerned... is this...

HS: We would like to gently remind you that is your name for us.

DENNY: Well, are you representative of Light Beings? Are you part of the Light of Consciousness?

HS: You may associate us with whatever you desire. We can tell you that basically the answer to your question is yes. And there will be different perceptions of what we are depending on through whom we are invited to manifest. In this case we associate through this channel and his belief system, which has changed somewhat from the time of our first contact until this time. But in general we are best described as being the Voice of Spirit, the most Holy of Spirits, the step between your mind and the Mind of God. We are the connecting link between you and your full Divinity.

DENNY: I was thinking of angels and I was thinking that they are what carry us across the Great Divide to God.

HS: Yes. Well, we are angels in your concept of that description and we are here to assist you. We thrive when given the opportunity to do this good work, which we wait patiently to do until the invitation is issued. It's not as if we did not exist from the beginning of this channel's existence. It's just that we waited patiently to receive our invitation to relate in this most intimate of manners. And we wait in the hearts of all mankind for that day of awakening when each and every individual calls upon us to assist them in the completion.

DENNY: That is very similar to what I've read about the ascended master concept.

HS: The lessons are presented in as many ways as there are people to receive.

DENNY: Yes.

I have some questions about the idea of a Light Body, but I'm not sure what my question is.

HS: Do you care to know if you have a Light Body?

DENNY: Yes.

HS: Yes.

DENNY: And this idea of ascension...the idea of Jesus, The Christ ascending from the tomb...

HS: Ascension is not actually rising anywhere or going anywhere. Ascension is an idea construct once again that has to do with perception and how you choose to perceive who you are and what your connection is with God, Goddess, All That Is. An ascended master, so to speak, is a consciousness that has fully realized his magnificent presence and its relationship to all of entirety.

DENNY: So, getting out of our own way, such as removing the struggling ego self and allowing the voice within to be our guiding beacon, is a way to open up to manifesting that presence?

HS: We would add another concept for your consideration: the realizations you have just expressed have come from that aspect of us that lives within you. We experience it much as completion of a circle...where it is almost as if we are having a dialogue with ourselves. We have come full circle in speaking through the two of you in one voice with different tones.

☉

We learned more about the nature of "The We" when a group of our close friends gathered in Sedona, Arizona. "The We" were invited to share with the group.

HS: Our way of being of service is to act as the third aspect of the Trinity. So, those of you who are familiar with the Father, the Son, and the Holy Ghost know who the Father is and know who the Son is. God, Goddess, All That Is is the Father. You, male or female, are the Son. We are the Holy Ghost. We are the Spirit. We are the connection. We are the link between you and your Father. We are the bridge between you and your Creator. We are the link that will help you complete your destiny. We are always available and that doesn't have anything to do with the current experience of the delivery of this message through this body at this time. Spirit—we who are here now, is always here whether this vocal chord or this body is expressing it or is available to express it or not. We, the Spirit and the message, are available always as long as you exist. We have always been and will always be the connection between you and the Creator. With your invitation we will assist you in completing your connection and your destiny...and that's why we offer always our unconditional love and our connection as a bridge to your Creator.

We do not have an agenda for you. We are your life coaches through eternity. We do not set your agenda. Your Higher Self sets your agenda. We offer our assistance for your completion.

◎◎

Then came the turn of the century. Denny and I were maturing. Our consciousness was expanding. The more we dialogued with "The We," the more we seemed to grow in awareness. And as we grew, their answers evolved and the information moved to higher and higher levels. In January of 2000 "The We" engaged in this non-stop soliloquy.

HS: We are here to take advantage of this opportunity to share with you what we believe is a simple, uncomplicated understanding for humans in the twenty-first century of the relationship between man and God.

First, to clarify and identify who we are: We are the Voice of Spirit. The Holy Voice of Spirit. The connection between God, Goddess, All That Is, and the Son. The connection between the Father and the Son is the Holy Spirit—the Holy Ghost as written about in the Bible.

We feel the time has come in the twenty-first century that scientific discovery is presenting a description of reality that makes it very clear that all of existence is both wave and particle. Quantum physics is recognizing that when man observes creation it physicalizes as matter and is scientifically identified as particle. When one tries to measure it under microscopic conditions the elements that make up matter (the quantum) are not an object. They cannot be measured. They are both wave and particle. Things exist in wave form until they are observed. When they are observed they solidify and become particles. They become matter.

The relationship between God, Goddess, All That Is and the Son is the symbolic representation of this inner reality. God, being non-physical, is the wave. God's creation, created in His image and likeness, is also merely a wave; consciousness created by the Supreme Source of Consciousness. In entering into physicality, a separation occurs as that consciousness observes itself and that is the very act of physicality.

When the Bible indicates that man is created in the image of God, it simply means that consciousness (in the wave form that is God)... is also what man is in his true nature. The illusion of physicality is created by the separation of the creation observing itself.

⊚⊚

Over the years our time spent with "The We" has varied from constant and intense to sporadic. There have been times when we would conduct more than one channeling session in a day. At other times we'd converse with "The We" daily for several weeks at a time. And of course, there were also times that weeks or months would go by without our initiating any contact. It's interesting to note that we never initiated contact without getting the response, "We are here." This unique source of information has never once declined our invitation to speak.

Even at one point after not having chatted with "The We" for over a year and a half, when we invited their presence, there they were, ready to resume communication.

HS: We are here and we bid you greetings and we welcome with enthusiasm this opportunity to be with you. We recognize much time has transpired for you since our last visit. We however, have no perception of the passage of time for we operate in the Now Moment, which is infinite and everlasting. How may we be of service to you?

DENNY: I have questions regarding the information I have been reading in a book from The I Am Foundation. It concerns the inner workings of the Beings of Light and I am wondering what light you can shed on this teaching?

HS: We will shed light on the Light.

(Laughter.)

This is Consciousness Light. We offer for your consideration the idea that all there is...is consciousness. It is from consciousness that all reality springs. You are actually engaging in, from our perspective, an exercise in futility if you try to compartmentalize consciousness... for all is consciousness. It is all consciousness and all manifestation is an aspect of consciousness. So...you are consciousness. We are consciousness. The Beings of Light are consciousness. And all are manifestations of the same Oneness of God, Goddess, All That Is. So it is somewhat like looking at your hand and trying to label the first finger as one concept and the second finger as a different concept when they all belong to the same hand.

Now there are different degrees of experience with different degrees of consciousness. Since your mind creates entirely what you experience, you can have connections with whatever aspect of consciousness your heart desires. If your question to us is are these Light Beings real? The answer is yes. They are real expressions of consciousness as are all the other expressions of consciousness that you choose to experience. Your choice in the matter is what is of significance because you have the facility to act as a filtering system for what you become aware of...and it all has to do with where you put your focus of attention and what beliefs you bring with you. Those beliefs become the filters through which your experiences are perceived.

For example...if you have a concept of Light Beings that is somewhat different than your husband's concept of Light Beings, you will have one experience with those Light Beings. He will have another experience, or possibly no experience of those Light Beings, depending on his focus of attention and their acceptability in the framework of his belief system.

DENNY: If my attention is placed on the unfolding of a perfect life or God perfection...instead of my focusing on what isn't working or what isn't right...then will that not draw forth into this consciousness perfection itself?

HS: This life is perfection itself. Your perception of

it can vary, depending on what attributes of your own consciousness you allow to come forth. If you come forth in judgment of things being less than perfect, that will be your reality for that moment.

DENNY: If my attention is placed on God Self unfolding moment to moment, then won't that create around me God Self unfolding moment to moment?

HS: Yes. And God Self is unfolding moment to moment about you in the co-creation of the life you experience from the point of view that you create your own reality simultaneously with all the other beings creating their own realities...and without them bumping into or colliding with each other.

DENNY: Well it seems to me that we have learned in this society to live with struggle...doubt...fear...shame... and negativity.

HS: All of those things do exist in your reality, yes. And they are all products of beliefs that you have held at one time or another. And those beings in your reality having similar experiences have held similar beliefs in whatever shape, manner, or form they occur, distinctively from one being to another.

DENNY: This is probably because we teach our incoming young people to believe in a whole concept of reality based on separation.

HS: And we would ask, why do you do that? Why not do it a different way?

DENNY: That's what I'm beginning to see. We have options. We have choices. We can begin to teach the perfection of the moment.

HS: That is the teaching we have always advocated and

the highly evolved beings of your physical reality have taught in this manner as well. There are also numerous non-physical consciousnesses that are teaching the same information in non-physical ways to many people on your planet.

DENNY: I'm not wanting to get hung up on any one way to be, and at the same time I am looking at the new principles that are coming into my consciousness.

HS: There is no "one way" to be. The perfection of existence is the understanding that all ways of being are valid and can be integrated into the common human experience. Your process now is commendable and exciting because you are fulfilling your destiny by making very specific choices about what kind of reality you prefer. You are finding more opportunities to consciously create the reality you prefer. In that process we would caution you not to get too stuck in excluding certain situations and circumstances that could be included somewhere in your realm. In other words, it all is valid. You do not want to waste energy on eliminating something. That is nearly an impossible task because you would have to create a void in the universe to accomplish that. And your power can be used so much more effectively in other avenues rather than creating the void that would be necessary to eliminate things you find distasteful. So, allow for the validity of those distasteful things and put them somewhere beyond your immediate scope of involvement, but allow for their validity in the universe.

DENNY: Yes, yes...not to eliminate them, but also not to focus on them. To focus instead on the reality I prefer. But there's something larger coming through, a larger picture of the reality I prefer is beginning to emerge that would include within it some of the abilities of the great teachers who have been here on our planet. I'm thinking of Sai Baba and his ability to bring forth objects from nothing and make them manifest in an instant. Perhaps that may be something that all of us can do. I hadn't even considered that.

HS: Well consider that all things are possible. You have been told that from the beginning of time, even in the writing in your Bible and before that. All things are possible. We would like you to remember, in looking at the life and activities of Sai Baba, he has a great accumulation of knowledge. He has great power to the point of being able to manifest and create, yet Sai Baba chooses to embrace the fact that some people have chosen to experience poverty. Do you think he would not be able to change that status for them as simply as he manifests a trinket? He understands it is their Higher Self's choice to have the experience of poverty...of which he has no right to re-configure.

DENNY: But if a person in poverty calls to his Higher Self for a change of that condition, would not such a thing be possible?

HS: Yes. Each being's sovereignty includes the choice to create a different reality at any point in time...as you recognize time to exist.

DENNY: Which is recognizing this idea of an "I Am" presence...a Higher Power...a reaching up for the Light of Consciousness in everything that is manifest.

HS: And please do remember you are your Higher Power. It is not somebody else you are appealing to. You are not searching outward. You are turning inward to the recognition of the magnificence of your being.

DENNY: I have another question. What's the connection between you, "The We," and the Oneness?

HS: We are you and you are we and we are One.

DENNY: Then is it true that individual consciousness, such as I am at this point in time, is just not in touch with the larger aspect—which includes you as well as all?

HS: We would address your question by reminding you that you are the total universe. You are the center from which all is manifest. You have created everything in your reality including this relationship which you are now experiencing. So, even though words and voice appear to come from the person next to you...their origin is, in fact, within your consciousness. There is only the One Consciousness.

DENNY: Yes. Consciousness itself is the Oneness.

HS: Yes. God, Goddess, All That Is, whatever name you give it, it is one singular dynamic of multifaceted manifestation.

DENNY: So, what's up with my friend Sperry who promotes this Oneness Theory? What's up there?

HS: One more manifestation of the One Consciousness of All That Is.

DENNY: And he reflects back to Ron and me our unowned light shadow, or higher aspect, or something?

HS: Reflects as a mirror reflects whatever is its true reality. There is that that is. And it is so multifaceted that for your comprehension and appreciation of it, it must be reflected in tiny increments in that you focus your attention on this particular aspect of the reflection of the totality of all that is. From moment to moment your focus of attention comes like a laser in experiencing another aspect of all that is, but in human or physical experience you have a limited ability to experience All That Is. And so, you experience it in bits and pieces as your focus moves from aspect to aspect of All That Is.

DENNY: Okay, then how can I learn to embody the larger perspective of the Oneness? How do I wake up?

HS: You are awake. You may have the desire to experience more fully your universe and that is certainly possible simply by allowing yourself to come fully into the present moment and as you become fully present, you expand your awareness. You break down the barriers of limited perspective by being more fully present in the moment so that your consciousness is not distracted or diminished, but is filling all of the "here and nowness" of your experience.

All limitations are self-imposed, so by coming to total presence here and now the limitations that confine your perspective diminish and the being is then able to experience more fully its existence.

DENNY: I'm thinking about the narrowed down focus of the Now Moment—the laser beam aspect of that focus....

HS: It is not a matter of narrowing down, but expanding it out as you come totally and fully into the present.

DENNY: Well it looks to me as though it narrows down really small and in that small moment it expands to fill everything.

HS: You tend in physicality to narrow down your focus from point to point and from moment to moment. The more presence you can bring to the moment, the more fully you experience.

III

Creating Your Reality

To understand ourselves better, we discovered it was helpful to stay focused on one of the most important aspects of this new teaching. That is the concept that Consciousness comes first: we create our own reality, and we do it through our thoughts and beliefs. Life experiences do not come "at" us, they come from us.

In July of 1996, during my first public channeling for an audience that went beyond the customary one or two close friends in attendance, "The We" laid down a number of fundamental principles about consciousness and creating our own reality that helped us understand ourselves better.

You Create Your Own Reality

HS: We are here and we are very pleased to be with the number of people who have made an effort to bring themselves to this environment where Spirit is encouraged to come forth.

It is helpful, we feel, for you to understand that there

is a vastness to your being that not only are you unable to comprehend, but we are unable to define fully for you at this time. We wish to provide certain little nudges this evening that could move you in a direction that allows for the possibility that maybe some of these concepts are so. We urge you in the days to come to reflect on some of the principles that will be put forth tonight and set aside your old beliefs and allow that "maybe it's so—that you do create your own reality, that you are not victims, that your life is symbolic." We would point out that many people accept the significance of dreams. We would ask you to look at books that have been written discussing the symbolism of dreams. If you can accept that things that happen in your dreams are representations of inner realms, then why not also believe that the events in your physical, waking existence are also symbolic and have great meaning on the inner plane?

Nothing happens by accident. There is a sacredness to each relationship in your life...whether it is someone you feel to be friend or foe. Your enemies are your greatest teachers. If you take the opportunity to explore what they represent, what they symbolize, then your learning can be accelerated. Your purpose here is one of self-realization. Your goal is not only to realize your potential and to explore fully the vastness of your multi-dimensionality—but also to learn to love every aspect of yourself and that can allow you then to love others.

We would like to make one other recommendation at this point: that you consider there are only two powers in the universe. One is love and the other is fear. They cannot exist simultaneously. You will be amazed at what you will learn in regard to symbols in your life and relationships and experiences if you recognize that you have an opportunity in every situation to choose love or to choose fear. Sometimes it is not clearly apparent to you when fear is here, but we remind you if it is not love it is fear and that can be your early warning system to explore further what it is a fear of, and to recognize what its purpose is in your life.

There Is No Objective Reality

Most of us have been taught to believe that there is something called objective reality—that there is one "right way" to perceive. From the very beginning of contact with "The We," Denny and I began receiving insights about ourselves and about human behavior, especially about the subjectivity of reality. We have come to realize that everything we witness and experience "out there" is taken "in here"—into our individual minds, and is subjected to our individual interpretations and judgments of good and bad, based on our personal experiences, preferences, and beliefs. There is no such thing as the one and only "way it is."

HS: You exist from moment to moment to moment. The idea that some things are "work" and some things are "play" are superficial designations that you have put upon your own existence. Existence cannot be compartmentalized. Existence is. It just is.

DENNY: Yes. I've learned that the only meaning anything has is the meaning we assign to it.

HS: Think in terms of life being filled with symbols that represent your inner reality. It might be helpful to consider the experience you have when you are on vacation. You're familiar with the zeal, the enthusiasm that comes from embracing the positive perspective that accompanies being on vacation. There's a good feeling, a sense of joy and adventure and excitement that comes with being on vacation. That's why you call vacations "recreation," because you are recreating a symbolic environment that is in keeping with the positive reality you prefer. And it may help people who are just beginning to grasp the idea that you create your own reality to take a look at the difference between vacation or recreation time and the time they classify as their work time.

Now it is true that some people go on vacation and have a lousy time, and there are some people who go to work and have a joyous time. Both people are creating their reality through their thoughts and beliefs. Those who have a joyous time at work are creating that positive reality because of their joy and enthusiasm for what they do at work.

Change Your Mind, Change Your Reality

In September of 2000 I became fascinated with a news item that was part of my evening radio shift on San Francisco's all news station KCBS. I found myself reading the following introduction to a story filed by one of my colleagues who had interviewed a prominent California psychiatrist, a doctor who has done some of the most extensive brain scan research in the world.

Here's what I read: "You can improve the condition of your heart with exercise. You can reduce the risk of cancer through diet, and now comes evidence that you can physically alter your brain with your thoughts or feelings. Here's the story from KCBS reporter Rebecca Corral."

CORRAL: "Researchers at the University of Iowa hooked patients to brain imaging equipment and asked them to think about something very sad, or something that made them angry, or an especially joyful event, like a wedding or the birth of a baby. The resulting scans detected changes in the brain's blood flow and chemistry. Fairfield, California, psychiatrist Dr. Daniel Amen is one of the pioneers in this field. He's seen dramatic physical changes in the before and after scans of patients who'd been through a life crisis."

DR. AMEN: "Sometimes we'll do the study with people thinking about different things and when you think sad thoughts your brain actually takes on the pattern that we correlate with clinical depression. When you think happy thoughts, hopeful thoughts, your brain takes on a much healthier state. If you can train your brain to think more positively, psychiatrists use the term cognitive therapy— therapy for your thoughts, it actually has an impact on healing your brain. So, just because you're depressed doesn't mean necessarily you need medicine. Sometimes psychotherapy can be extremely helpful to the actual functioning of your brain..."

After hearing that news report I did a channeling session and asked "The We" to help me better understand the human mind and brain. Here's what they had to say:

HS: We are here. What we offer today may provide some

clarity on the mind-body connection and how consciousness functions on the physical plane. Existence, consciousness, beingness expresses through humanity via the mind, using the brain as the physical apparatus or tool for expression and manifestation.

The mind, however, is shared, so that your human experience is subject to two masters working within that one mind. The two masters work with the total consent and cooperation of the human being who has the absolute power to choose which will be allowed to take center stage and be supported in creating and perceiving all physical experience.

The Higher Self or Divine Self aspect of Consciousness lovingly extends itself through the mind, giving birth to thought, which triggers feelings, which manifest as the creation of your experience in physical reality. Divine Self knows only truth and love, for that is what it is.

As human beings you allow Divine Mind to be shared with ego or personality mind...that which denies the Oneness and creates the illusion of separation. When ego is allowed to control the mind, the illusion of separation appears real, which allows for fear, doubt, and sin. But we would remind you: you always have the power of choice. It is your choice that determines what you experience. Will you choose to make Self the master of your mind, or will you choose to allow ego to run your mind and thereby run your life? You make the choice...the choice for love or fear... the choice for truth or illusion...the choice for oneness or separateness.

In other words...science and spirit are speaking the same truth. With thoughts of love and joy and hope the mind, using the physical apparatus called brain, produces a set of physical circumstances, which your scientists now have the instruments to measure, that are life affirming, nurturing and healthy to the body.

With thoughts of hatred, anger, and frustration that same brain causes a totally different set of physical reactions and a completely different set of responses in the body in terms of disharmony, energy imbalances and other chemical reactions that can potentially escalate from disharmony to dis-ease.

Change your thoughts: change your brain. Change your brain: change your reality and change your life.

The decision is, always has been, and always will be yours. In your conscious mind you choose which master to put in charge. You choose to see through the eyes of love, or through fear.

☯

On another occasion "The We" informed us:

HS: You are everything. You are all of creation. You are every dimension simultaneously. You put your attention here now and that is what creates your physicality, but that does not negate your existence in all other places of creation—even though as you sit here now you are not aware of existence in all those other places in creation. We would remind you that you are creating everything in this room in your own private universe. The person sitting next to you is doing the same thing and in that way you co-create this reality to experience each other. Because you are part of each other's dream, you are one. You are the creator. You are also all the characters in your creation, as is the person sitting next to you and everyone in this room. And when you go to the deepest part of yourself, you all go to the same place.

You will always create whatever it is you hold most prominent in your consciousness. You will always get everything you want and everything you don't want, so be mindful of where you put your focus and know that right and wrong and good and bad simply do not exist. It is a judgment that you have laid on top of what has been created.

IV

Inner Basics

In the years that we've been learning from "The We," great emphasis has been placed on the existence of an inner reality. Originally having no clue as to what that meant, we gradually came to appreciate that there are inner basics, or aspects of ourselves that create the world of physical reality that we experience. "The We" have provided a map of this inner world to help us understand how we create symbolic reflections of our inner reality in the outer world.

Often we don't even know what that inner reality is. It is by learning to look at our reflections in the outer world that we get a better idea of what's going on within us.

We have learned that when we become more conscious and are willing to drop our negative interpretation of events, we simultaneously stop sabotaging ourselves and allow life to flow. When we do this we accelerate our spiritual growth and realize the potential to find a gift in every experience.

Consciousness

On December 4, 1999, during a gathering with several friends at our home, "The We" shared a view of the inner dimensions of consciousness. During this channeling an interesting situation occurred that affected everyone present. We had all become comfortable in front of a lovely fire in our living room, which may have had something to do with what everyone experienced...or it may have been more than that.

HS: We would like to share with all of you the various dimensions of your consciousness. The idea is that thought is something you are extremely familiar with, in that you can always count on many, many, many thoughts occupying your mind and your time. If you step outside of thought for a moment there will be feelings behind those thoughts. And we encourage you to take this journey, as it is the next step toward going within and having a more profound experience of who you are.

And once you quiet the thoughts and experience the feelings...the next step is to journey into the area of beliefs that have formed those feelings that have then created those thoughts.

And so, we encourage you, as a method of developing spiritually, to find the time to search your belief systems and become more aware of what those beliefs are that you have adopted without great thought or scrutiny.

Next, beyond or further into your wonderful selves... beyond beliefs...you will find an area of knowingness. And this knowingness will be a revelation to you. You will, when you're able to be still and know, learn some revolutionary and startling things about who you are and how your universe works.

Then, beyond knowingness is the essence of who you are and that is simply the Self...the Beingness...the center of who you are. So there is this grand area of consciousness for you to explore in your journey of Self discovery that says you do not need to play just on the edges of thought, you can go much deeper into yourself for an experience of rich and nourishing understanding of who you are and how you play your part in All that Is.

Thought > Feeling > Belief > Knowingness > Beingness (Silence and a long pause.)

HS: We didn't mean to stun you.

(Group laughter.)

DENNY: You knocked everybody out. This whole room fell asleep. Oh my God!

Understanding Ourselves

In nearly every session with "The We," we have been gently guided to a deeper understanding of who we are and what our relationship is to God or Source. Over time the mysteries of life began to clarify as we were offered a new perspective on reality.

FEMALE: Could you explain to me what the God Force means?

HS: We are consciousness in a non-physical way. We are connected to the channel's consciousness. We are also connected to your consciousness. We are connected to all consciousness in a magnificent manner. The interconnectedness is the expression of God...All That Is. The force, the energy that is us is God, is you, is all One. God is manifest through each human spirit, each tree spirit, each flower and fish and animal spirit. All things in physicality have consciousness. Even a rock has consciousness. That consciousness is the connection to the God Force. There is confusion in the religions that create God in man's image. Man is truly created in God's image and is far more than the physical bodies you're currently wearing in this lifetime. That part of you that exists beyond death, that vast consciousness of which your physical experience is only a small part, that vast consciousness is the inner connection with all other consciousness. If you follow that idea out far enough it takes you to God, Goddess, All That Is.

Do you ever have the experience of reading another person's mind? It happens most frequently with people who are strongly connected by their love for one another. That situation of reading someone's mind is simply working the connection through the grid work that allows you to understand what that person is thinking because you are...we are all interconnected. Your physical focus often prevents you from recognizing the connection. You don't always read minds because physicality is a filtering system that is actually keeping many energies and unseen factors out of your center of focus. Every now and then when you transcend the focus of the physical you open those doorways to sharing thoughts and pictures and feelings with others.

JIM: "The We" talks about symbolism. I'm trying to understand how our external realities are symbolic of what's going on inside us...in our inner life.

HS: Usually unresolved issues in your inner life and

areas that have not been fully accepted become "in your face," so to speak. And to varying degrees, if ignored they can escalate. It's like Spirit demands to be heard and will sound an alarm in a gentle manner, hoping that you will respond. And if you don't, Spirit will use a two-by-four, if necessary, to get your attention.

We would like to remind you that one of your first creations (in creating your own reality) is the creation of your body. You have a body because of your consciousness. Your consciousness has created your body. Your body becomes diseased and symptoms appear that need your attention when certain things are not in harmony within you. How severe the ailment becomes depends on your willingness or unwillingness to alter your course in life as to what you do and what you believe.

Forgetting Your Story

While "The We" say that we create our bodies, they continually remind us we are *not our bodies,* and furthermore, we are *not our stories* and they caution against getting too attached to either one.

What are our personal stories? It took a little time for us to understand the concept of having personal stories. We struggled to recognize that there were times when we interpreted the behavior of others or cast ourselves in the role of either hero or victim as we interpreted events and experiences in the struggle to understand our lives. Becoming conscious of our inner dialogue and separating ourselves from that "play-by-play announcer in our minds" was quite challenging. It was difficult to see that those interpretations were not the reality we thought they were. We began to learn to pay attention to which master we were putting in charge of our minds: Spirit or ego.

Some of our most profound learning came through recognizing the difference between love and fear, reality and illusion. "The We" continually challenged us to recognize "our stories," and to subject our stories to inquiry in a search for truth.

FEMALE: How do you forget your story or undo your story?

HS: The mind has two masters and you choose which one to put in control. When the Voice of Spirit is allowed, you will be assisted in clearly seeing through the illusion. When ego is chosen to preside, the mind will fabricate a story, forget that it has fabricated the story, buy the illusion as fact and forget what is real.

Only what the Creator created is real. All else is illusion. Only what the Creator created is lasting, eternal, love. All else is illusion. That means fear is an illusion. Fear is a misperception. True perception fosters love. True perception, discerning between the reality and the illusion, fosters love.

So when you find yourself experiencing fear you may want to ask yourself, "If fear is a misperception, and if it's my choice, what might I choose that would be closer to the truth? What might I choose that would dispel the fear and would bring me closer to love?"

Does that make sense?

FEMALE: I'll have to wait until the situation arises.

HS: You might find it interesting to begin giving some

thought to what stories are driving your life right now. And the best way to get a lead on that is to ask, "What frightens me?"

Old beliefs do not die easily, so this awakening may not happen overnight, but if you continue in frightened moments to recall that fear is a misperception, and if you remember that you have a choice...then brother choose again. Choose love, not fear. And in the next Now Moment that fear appears, choose love again, and choose love again. It's a matter of diligence.

FEMALE: Choosing to love yourself?

HS: Love of yourself is the ultimate choice, of course.

FEMALE: Being a perfectionist?

HS: Is being a perfectionist love? Or is being a perfectionist being critical and unaccepting...

FEMALE: That's right.

HS:...and holding judgments? We would always urge each and every one of you to lay your judgments aside because you don't have all the facts to make the judgment. So as good as you think your judgments are, they miss the mark because you simply don't have the big picture.

FEMALE: I feel like I'm in an altered state. I'm totally focused on what "The We" is saying. I'm not sleepy, but....

HS: Yes. There is, emanating from the channel, an energy of peaceful and serene calmness that you are all able to entrain with and come to this still point where knowing awaits.

It's all right if you don't have questions. When the mind is truly stilled there are no questions. There is nothing to do, there is simply being.

So we would suggest that you enjoy your altered state—

that you enjoy the stillness. And remember at a future time that you are able to produce that state of calm and there will be times when the world is once again with you, and the stories are flying fast and furious, and you may want to take time out and come back to creating this place of perfect peace.

FEMALE: But I don't feel like I created it. I feel more like I tuned in to it, so I'm not sure how to do it again on my own.

HS: Both are true. You are never not creating your reality. You create your reality one hundred percent of the time. So yes, you have created this situation in this Now Moment to have this enlightened experience.

FEMALE: I'll take it.

HS: We send you our unconditional love.

DENNY: You knocked everybody out again.

HS: Yes, from time to time in moments like these people have a rare opportunity to go to what is referred to as "the void," out of which all creation is born. So relish and enjoy the moment. Know that there is nothing to do. Know that you can pick up your story at any time and go back into the world and do the things you need to do—have your shopping lists and your work projects, your agendas and itineraries. But know that you are more than your story and there is a fullness and richness and a depth to your being that you can nurture and experience again at those times when you need a respite, an oasis, a centering, healing situation.

FEMALE: There is nothing but the now. That's what I'm getting in touch with.

HS: That's correct. That's all there ever is...forever.

The awareness of Spirit, welcomed into your life in this Now Moment by your invitation, heals, creates, connects you with your Creator, and brings you joy and awareness of love. It's an opportunity as you sit here with your fellow beings not only to recognize the Christ within you, but the Christ within everyone.

Sabotaging Oneself, Not Letting Life Flow

On more than one occasion "The We" reminded us of the importance of allowing life to flow through us. It's amazing how often we sabotage ourselves by blocking the natural flow of life. How often are we humans doing instead of humans being?

FEMALE: How do I get out of my own way to allow my life to flow more and Spirit to come through me more?

HS: Perhaps it would help you to remember it is simply an awareness of that that is. There is nothing to do. It is a matter of trusting and having faith that you can just be without figuring or willing or doing or working. Allow. Allow with the awareness and the trust and faith that you are perfection. All aspects of your life are perfection and in Divine order. The only thing that disturbs that is your ego mind which is not able to see the perfection and will try to convince you that what you are experiencing at any moment of your life, from the ego standpoint, is a problem or something less than a Divine representation of your soul's growth. In other words, every experience is a blessing. Every experience has meaning, giving you an opportunity to self-realize another aspect of your Divine being.

And so there really isn't a whole lot to do, other than relaxing the notion that you have to stay busy or work hard or do something other than allow for the presence of Spirit in your life.

If you would like a manual that includes some "To Do's" we would suggest that the "to do" be that you ask Spirit, moment to moment to moment, to tell you where to go, whom to see, and what to say.

FEMALE: So are you suggesting we have continuous dialogue with Spirit, or putting that out and then being quiet, allowing Spirit to speak?

HS: We would come back to the suggestion that it is helpful to be still and know. The "be still" part is a way of turning off the ego mind. The command "be still" puts to rest some of the chatter that comes from the ego part of your mind. "Know" is the second step that allows you to open to what comes forth through your heart in the way of wisdom and guidance. "Be still and know." Allow and listen and observe. You will physically feel the peace and love and joy that comes from that stillness. And from that stillness emerges the knowledge, the knowingness, the beingness that can replace the doingness. You are human beings...you are not humans doing.

DENNY: You said there's nothing to do, just to be. That sounds like a way of accessing your life purpose. Can we just step out of the way and allow ourselves to be guided?

HS: You can do anything you want to do. You are existing in a freewill universe. There are no regulations. God doesn't step in and say, "You can't do that." God loves you so much that He allows absolute total and free choice in every aspect of your life.

DENNY: I'm thinking, if you're looking for a job the "doing" is going to the want ads and reading the newspaper. Is the "being" looking for a prompting?

HS: You can do whatever you feel you need to do to be a responsible and productive person. You can set goals for a day, for a month, for the next year or for your whole life. You can do whatever you think will assist in furthering you to your goal. Just know that it's a bit of an illusion. There is a greater part of yourself that assists in the manifestation of your life experience from moment to moment to fulfill the purpose of your Higher Self. Your Higher Self has an agenda that is for your greater good and it will keep all of these things on your agenda regardless of what you do or don't do. You can have a much easier life experience by getting in agreement with those things rather than resisting those things.

FEMALE: I'm confused. You can have an easier time of it by getting in the flow, rather than resisting what things?

HS: It's a bit like riding a horse. You can ride the horse in the direction it's going more easily than you can by trying to change the direction or ride in the opposite direction. The Higher Self is kind of like the horse, in that it has laid out a route for your life and you can flow with that or be in resistance to that.

That is not to say that you can't have desires and plans. But at the same time, part of your being can trust: number one that you have a Higher Self; number two that your Higher Self has your greater good in mind at all times; and number three that your Higher Self is on an unseen level, orchestrating events in your life for the fulfillment of your purpose and grander scheme.

We are simply reminding you that working in harmony with the Higher Self, riding the horse in the direction it's going rather than efforting or resisting or being out of balance, can greatly enhance your life experience.

FEMALE: So the Higher Self is assisting us along the route or the journey, kind of giving us the direction?

HS: You have available to you more assistance than you can possibly imagine. You are thoughts in the mind of God. You have guardian angels and guides who are always with you, always overseeing your soul's growth. We lovingly remind you that your soul growth may be different than your human growth, your personality growth, your ego-influenced growth. Your Higher Self, the part of your soul that is connected to God, is assisted by Divine Masters and angels and guardians from all levels of consciousness, whether you are aware of them or not—whether you see them or not.

The ego part of your mind is not making it easy for you. The ego will remind you that this is reality. The physical solid world is what is. We would remind you that is not reality. That is the illusion. Reality is what is eternal. There is nothing in this room that is eternal other than the essence of each Spiritual Being here. You Spiritual Beings are here in human bodies for only a short time. Your human bodies will die. Your physical manifestations of matter will not last. In time they will crumble. That's because they are illusion. You—you will last forever. You are the reality. You did not create yourself. You were created by God. What God created is lasting, eternal, reality. All else is illusion.

(Long silence.)

HS: Good. Be still and know. Sit with the silence. Stop thinking for a moment. Just sit with the silence.

Know that God is love and you, made in his image, are love and you are Divine and eternal. And there is so much more to you than your body or your mind. And know that you have our unconditional love always and forever. You are all in the perfect place, doing the right thing, at the right time and we encourage you to hold on to that memory in the coming hours, days, and weeks when ego mind tries to convince you otherwise.

How to Accelerate Spiritual Growth

The more we talked to "The We" and began to practice their teachings in our daily life, the more our focus changed. It was not uncommon for the dialogue to turn to esoteric questions of enlightenment, higher consciousness, and spiritual awareness. Many of the people, both friends and strangers, who came to engage in conversation with "The We" were becoming spiritual seekers.

FEMALE: One more question. Is there a possibility for me in this lifetime to reach a state of wholeness, higher awareness or consciousness?

HS: Absolutely. You are in a state of wholeness and peace. The question would be are you willing to accept the existence of your state of wholeness and peace?

FEMALE: Yes. Is there nothing to do?

HS: We are suggesting that it's not something that needs to be achieved. It is merely something that needs to be recognized. You already exist wholly and completely and you exist in a state of peace and harmony. Your degree of lack is simply your lack of recognition of the perfection of your life. This is offered not in criticism or in any manner other than the greatest degree of love and compassion for your human struggle, which our non-physical consciousness recognizes as being a challenging event. And we know that you are capable of rising to a higher vibrational perspective of your life experience at any given moment.

FEMALE: Is the frequency in which we vibrate manifested in the body?

HS: Your body is just one aspect of your consciousness's manifestation. You are consciousness...essence. Your beingness is first and foremost. Your physicality is an afterthought—a by-product of your consciousness. In consciousness and in physicality and in non-physicality you have vibratory frequencies that make you uniquely who and what you are—which differentiates you from other beings.

◎◎

In a separate session later with our friend Gemma, we learned more:

HS: We are here...We would remind you that we speak in many voices through many individuals. We function on the dimension of interconnected consciousness and our ability to help access information is always at your command.

GEMMA: Can we discuss things such as, what would accelerate our spiritual growth?

HS: Our suggestion would be, on a regular basis to

remember the truths that connect you to your inner reality as opposed to reacting to what you create in your outer, symbolic, physical reality.

One of those basic truths is you are Divine. Another is you are not a victim. You are in control. Your Higher Self is always functioning to assist in the creation of times and events for your greater purpose and the fulfillment of your life tasks.

In what area do you wish to see a change occur?

GEMMA: My understanding is that meditation is a very useful and important tool, but I don't like meditation. And when I do meditate, which has been every day now, I don't find that it's very useful.

HS: We would observe that there's no point in doing something that you do not enjoy. There is no purpose served in doing something because someone else has suggested it might be of benefit if you don't find a true warming of the heart from the experience. Perhaps you have a misconception of what it is to meditate. Perhaps you're trying to follow someone else's direction rather than finding in your heart the way to self-satisfying, nourishing, nurturing communication with Spirit.

We would suggest that meditation is whatever brings you close to the feeling of love and the warmth of Spirit. That could be looking at a flower, or simply clearing your mind and making room for God thoughts.

GEMMA: I've been trying to do Vipassana meditation. But I think it's not for me.

HS: We would invite you to quiet yourself. Take a few deep breaths. Allow thoughts to rise and release. Look to the moments, however brief they might be, between the thoughts and in an easy and enjoyable manner begin to appreciate and enjoy those brief moments of "non-thought."

Now, if you have to effort to do that, then it is self-defeating. So again, for you it is learning to allow... learning to distinguish between that natural, spontaneous unfoldment and working to perform a task.

GEMMA: Thank you.

Can I address another topic that I have a strong impulse to ask about?

HS: Yes. You should always follow your heart.

GEMMA: There's a saying that you'll never have more than you can handle...

HS: That is correct.

GEMMA: And I am confused because I also see people around me who can't handle some of the things in their lives. Some people go crazy or become physically or emotionally unable to handle things.

HS: It is not a matter of their being given more than they can handle. It is a matter of your inability to see with the larger perspective, from whence the gift came.

Things happen with a purpose for each and every person. We would like to remind you that it is always for a positive purpose, whether you can see it or not. For example, the person who goes crazy has an opportunity to assimilate important circumstances from his or her inner reality that need to be digested despite what the accepted customs of society may be. Rules of society and definitions of sanity are merely perspectives that are agreed upon by committee.

GEMMA: What I get hung up on is this notion that we should be able to see things from a different perspective...

HS: Would you repeat that?

GEMMA: A problem I have is in understanding that we're expected to see things...

HS: No. We asked you to repeat because it was our impression that you had a definition for how you were "expected to function" in this life. There are no expectations. Your experiences are created by a part of yourself. They are put into your reality by you, to provide opportunities for you to interrelate and make choices that give you the information you need to make future choices and gain the realization of who you are. As you grow and experience your lessons, it is always a free choice with no expectations.

We would ask you, who is responsible for defining what is expected of you? Where does the expectation come from?

GEMMA: Well...

HS: It may perhaps be a false notion that there are right and wrong ways to do things, or right or wrong ways to be.

There are no right and wrong ways from our perspective.

Finding the Gift

We were being told that everything was a blessing. Our challenge became finding the gift in every circumstance—even those situations that appeared to lack any redeeming blessing. The new millennium provided an unusual challenge in our home life. We can look back and laugh now, but at the time it seemed like the worst of the worst. Our septic tank stopped working, leaving us totally without bathroom facilities. Could "The We" possibly have a perspective on such a mundane experience? We couldn't begin to see a gift in this crappy event.

DENNY: I have a lot of questions. Seems that we have a lot going on in our lives. The septic tank is no longer working and it seems like it is symbolic of something. It also feels like an opportunity. Can you help clarify?

HS: We would observe that these are rich and fertile times for you and this is your opportunity to put your belief systems to the test of trust and truth. We recognize that degrees of difficulty are value judgments that your egos make in the day-to-day function of human life. We recognize that you also understand, but could be served by the reminder that all situations are fundamentally neutral. They only carry the judgment and interpretation that you place on them. So see if you can detach significantly from the opinions you have about the experience to understand that the process of dealing with the septic tank is no different than the process of any other event in your life. The negative judgment that comes forth is simply your unwillingness to be in agreement with the course of design your Higher Self has put forth for your growth and development.

DENNY: Well, nobody asked me. You know, like my Higher Self could have said, "Would you like this to happen?" No!

HS: You might spend some time searching for the beneficial aspects of this experience. We would suggest that it has given you an opportunity to re-experience philosophical beliefs. We suggest it has given you an opportunity to relate to others in a potentially positive way in simply commiserating and addressing the issue of re-designing your reality to have the circumstance shift from a challenge or a problem to be a completed and most satisfying past accomplishment.

There will come a time, if not at the present moment, when you will be able to feel great pride and satisfaction with the completion of the task at hand.

❀

In fact, we were blessed to have a young craftsman come to our rescue in our hour of need. Although he knew nothing about septic tanks, he knew a lot about a number of other construction matters. Not only was he brilliant, he was also a fast learner. He learned what was necessary to rebuild our old redwood septic tank, including renting and operating a back-hoe to dig new leach lines and everything else that was necessary to get our system up and operating. Although the process cost us several thousand dollars, he saved us many thousands more than if the project had been done by anyone else. This young man has become a close friend and a most trusted and valued contractor for dozens of remodeling projects over the years. The universe indeed gave us a magnificent gift with the experience of the broken septic tank.

V

Inner Struggles

We all have inner struggles. We all wish they would magically go away, but they don't. The best we can hope for is insight that allows us to view the struggle with consciousness. We were blessed to have "The We" as our personal source for understanding the meaning of our suffering.

We came to rely on the fact that "The We" was a source of intelligence that we could always count on for a fresh perspective. Our questions were continually met with wisdom and love. Over the years we relied more and more on this special guidance, whether the problem was out of the ordinary or routine. "The We" were always able to shed light on the situation by lovingly opening the door to a new point of view.

Depression

As a Marriage and Family Therapist, Denny is accustomed to sitting with people who struggle with unpopular feelings. Two of the most unpopular are

63

depression and anger. People don't like how either emotion feels. We would all much rather have ongoing joy and happiness. This is what makes the perspective of "The We" so challenging.

FEMALE: What about the depression I've been experiencing?

HS: Well, we see a full spectrum of available feelings and whereas you choose now to function in an area that you label as depression, you can move as easily and quickly on that line of emotions to less depression or more depression. You can move to the degree of despondency if you wish, or to the degree of minor irritation. Or you can even cross over the other side to slight bemusement at your circumstance or even to giddy laughter at the folly of it all.

The manner in which you experience any aspect of your life is one hundred percent a choice on your part and is never dictated by outside influences, powers, or anything beyond your ability to choose your experience.

Feeling Anger

When it comes to anger, many of us have been injured by the manner in which this feeling was expressed in our early years. This was true in my (Ron's) family of origin. Dad's anger would explode without limits. This would terrify Mom and us kids, so Mom made sure we all learned to "stuff" rather than express our anger. She thought she was teaching us the right way to deal with anger and how not to be like Dad. Having learned this behavior as a child, what "The We" said about anger was the last thing in the world I could have imagined.

FEMALE: I have anger. Is anger ever right?
HS: Anger is always right. Anger is an honest expression. Honesty is the same as love. Truth is the same as love. Fear is the opposite. So if you are truly angry, it is best not to deny it, but to express it. The danger comes when anger is repressed and eventually explodes in rage. Righteous anger is healthy and meaningful and is simply a means of communicating very clearly and uniquely to another being what your position is in a given situation. Repressed anger can erupt in a rage that injures and does harm. Anger will not do harm.

Struggling with One's Sexuality

Time and again in the course of these channeling sessions, we have seen people ask how to deal with their shortcomings or human characteristics that they find undesirable. A man who had been struggling with his bisexuality came for a session with "The We" and was curious about a physical condition that had been diagnosed as angina. He asked "The We" to shed light on the symbolic significance of the severe pain he had experienced for a number of years in his head and his chest. Here's what he learned.

HS: This symbolizes an incongruity between the head and the heart. You went through much of your life with your heart yearning for one kind of experience and your head telling you, "No, no, no, you shouldn't do that...or be that way...or think those thoughts."

Being able now to see the conflict in your life means you have taken a big step forward in understanding. This is the natural unfolding of your growth and self-actualization. You are beginning to recognize the symbols you have constructed in your life so that you can become aware of your beliefs.

MAN: I have been curious lately about some of my impulses and perhaps my own denial of an aspect of myself.

HS: A basic tenant for every human being is to come to an understanding of love; an understanding that love is all that matters. Love is primary to all other thoughts, beliefs, physical manifestations, idea constructs. Love is all there is.

The experience that you have chosen to create in this life is the way to lead you back to a basic experience of love and an understanding of love. This experience was needed and was chosen before birth to compensate for past experiences, in a prior lifetime, where your heart was not given voice. Your belief systems were so powerful in your last environment (incarnation) that love was very difficult for you to acknowledge, experience and appreciate. So, in this life, you have created an opportunity for feelings to be more powerful than intellect. And whether you recognize it or not, your life has been ruled by your feelings.

Is it not ironic that you have experienced this life thinking you are someone who does not feel, when in fact you feel so strongly that you fear it is out of your control? And so you grapple with feelings versus intellectual concepts. This incongruity between your mind and your heart manifests in your body—creating the pain in your chest and in your head.

Your lesson this life will be to understand and appreciate the difference between the intellectual process and the heart process and to learn to trust and follow your heart.

You can still play with, analyze, and discard or accept various forms of behavior. But you will do this despite what society or any other human being says is correct or proper. You will find within your heart that which makes sense to you.

To reiterate, it is your work this lifetime to learn to trust and accept your feelings. You are here to learn to love every aspect of yourself.

You have some difficulty accepting some of this material. You have difficulty accepting a new definition of reality. This is difficult for you to conceive because of your belief systems. Your old definitions of reality have such a strong hold on you that new concepts are unimaginable and unacceptable. The learning offered to you today is an opportunity to recognize that new ideas are often difficult to assimilate because of your old beliefs.

Changing Old Behavior Patterns

Denny and I made a huge leap in self understanding after a session in which "The We" encouraged us to become aware of the old behavior patterns or roles we had adopted in childhood to get our needs met. This was an "ah-ha" moment.

HS: We are here once again and we can give you some processes that can help people understand and release from the roles that they adopted in infancy which no longer serve them in adulthood.

Our reminder to you is that everything is love or a cry for love.

Human beings tend to function in such a manner that when they find something that works for them, they do it and do it and do it. If a little bit worked, more will work even better. So if being a good boy worked for the child, being a people pleaser should work for the adult. But there is no satisfaction in that. Wholeness comes not from giving up anything, but from embracing all of who you are in full love and appreciation.

Another example would be the person who over-cares. The same dynamic exists as with the over-pleaser. Caring got love in return. Caring more is expected to get more love…but at some point one gives up an aspect of oneself in over extending one's ability to care in a loving manner. When love goes out of the dynamic, everyone loses.

DENNY: I have a client like that who learned that being dependent and having other people tell her what to do was a way to…

HS: Get attention and companionship and support and love, as she defined love to be. And support for her survival.

"Take care of me. Take care of me. Prove you love me. Show me you love me by taking care of me."

DENNY: Yes, and it also includes "Tell me what to do and I will do it."

And now her husband tells her what to do and she

resents it because his old way of being turns out not to be better. It does not serve her. And the problem is not with her husband, the problem is with her because she's holding on to a role she's unconscious of and it no longer serves her.

HS: So once you assist someone in finding her role, a process can be used to release that person from the need to continue, out of habit, to seek love in that way. Offer her the opportunity to be as creative in finding a new expression of love as she was in creating the role in the first place in order to get love.

DENNY: Do you mean create another role?

HS: Create another way of expressing love. Everything is love or a cry for love, so if you are expressing love you won't be crying for love.

It's a shifting of consciousness on what you put out. The prior consciousness was centered on ways of taking in love through manipulation and finding false ways of getting something from someone.

DENNY: Yes, in her fear it was a call for love that she was not getting...not recognizing that the best way to get love is to generate the feeling within and to give it.

HS: Work through the heart and the connection with Higher Consciousness, allowing Spirit into your life to choose love over fear, to recognize truthfully how you can best express genuine love without making it artificial by over-extending or overdoing or over-achieving or over-caring.

DENNY: I have also worked with people who have just stopped doing anything. They've just stopped and been miserable. And I've seen that's the way they got what they needed when they were little kids. They just stopped and they didn't do anything. They just waited. Eventually somebody noticed them and took care of them. I can see the way now to help them break that old pattern. This could be so helpful to those people who are stuck in their "way of getting." If they can release it, they can learn to generate the feeling from within.

HS: It's a very important question to ask, how do you get your needs met? And it goes back a very, very long time to the earliest stages of life. Again, the false concept is: if that worked then, more of that will work even better now. But then you've run amuck.

DENNY: Thank you. Is there anymore you'd like to share?

HS: We would just remind you that we exist as part of your consciousness...the one consciousness that at its highest level is all interconnected. The answer is always available and always within. You are the total creator of your universe. We will always be available and of assistance in helping you through the maze that is ego created, to your connection with Self. Connection with Self can diminish some of the obstacles and confusion and help you touch again on truth. Remember, Truth and Love are one and the same.

Making Decisions

Often people struggle with making decisions. Even when people have learned the difference between ego and Spirit, it can still be difficult to distinguish them. One of the most frequently asked questions was how can we tell whether the voice is Spirit or ego?

FEMALE: I have a question. I frequently ask for guidance, but I have a hard time discerning when it's the voice of my personality or my ego or when it's the voice of my higher wisdom. I'm relating that to what you've said about love and fear. It's hard to discern that part.

HS: Is it possible that you are believing that "It's just my imagination?" When you're not certain of the validity of the voice within you, we would remind you to dispel your doubt by silencing the chatter. Tell the skeptical self to just hold on a minute and allow the voice of your heart to speak. A ring of truth will tell you which voice is the beneficial, nurturing, helpful voice to follow.

We have a sense that there's more here to explore and we encourage you perhaps to find an example of the confusion that troubles you in your life.

FEMALE: Well, this is a very simple and mundane one. I get very enthusiastic about something that is in front of me, but then it becomes kind of confusing to prioritize and then I get confused as to where these impulses are coming from because I get pulled in so many different directions.

HS: We would like to remind you that it is very helpful to stay in the Now Moment. It is good to ask yourself, "Now, at this moment, what is it that excites me the most?"

Given the answer to that question, in the next Now Moment pursue that without the judgment that says, "I should be doing something else...or maybe this isn't the one, maybe it's that one I should pursue."

You can have different choices in different Now

Moments. There's no reason if you select baking pies to satisfy your heart's desire that you have to bake pies for the rest of your life.

FEMALE: Well, with each of these excitements in my life there are commitments to other people and it becomes so involved that I feel reluctant to break those commitments.

HS: We feel that it may be helpful for you to understand that you cannot find true happiness by living by tribal rules or society's idea of what should give you satisfaction and fulfillment. You must take care of yourself first. You must protect your sovereignty. You must lead your life by your terms, not by other's expectations. That is not to say you need to be unkind to other people. That is not to say you hurt other people. But if you are true to yourself you can do it in such a way that you will feel good about what you agree to do, as well as what you don't do that other people think you should do. You will earn respect and find ways of lovingly taking good care of yourself.

FEMALE: Thank you. That's very helpful.

☯☯

On another occasion, "The We" clarified the decision making process with the following information.

FEMALE: How do you know whether it's love or fear when you feel you need to make decisions?

HS: Let us remind you dear one that you are not your story. You are not your body; you are not your sexual identity. You are certainly not your story. But, you have created all of these things for a specific purpose—to give you an arena in which to play that will further your understanding of yourself. So...recognize that the situation in front of you that confuses you is symbolic of situations that you are working out on an inner level. The way to tell whether it is the voice of fear or the voice of love is simply to ask yourself, "Is this love?"

Let us ask you, "Do you know what love feels like?"

FEMALE: Yes.

HS: We feel that all beings do know what love feels like when they still the chatter of their minds and look into their hearts. So remember what love feels like. Feel the feeling in your heart and if that is not the feeling you're experiencing then you'll know that the voice of fear has been raised again in your life. Then proceed more cautiously, more diligently. You can say, "Fear is here." You can make another choice. If it doesn't go away you can continue to play with and continue to reaffirm your desire to choose love. You can also call on us and the other unseen forces in the universe who are the defenders of love...and your call for help will always be answered.

VI

Two Forces

Human beings have two lenses available for viewing the world and their place in it. The question becomes, do we view the events of our lives through the eyes of love or fear? Becoming conscious of which filter we use enables us to alter our experience. Choosing to view life's experience through the lens of love puts us in greater contact with the love that is always present in every circumstance, whether we have the ability at the moment to see it or not. We are given the gift of free will. We absolutely always have the choice as to which filter we will use.

Love and Fear

On my birthday, January 21, 2000, "The We" emphasized the importance of understanding love and fear. What a present it was to receive this profoundly simple gift.

HS: We are here to clarify, reiterate and validate that you are the Son of God, created in His image. You are the co-creators that the Creator created.

The question was asked, "Is everything a projection?"

The answer is, there are two ways you create in physicality. One is by extension; the other is by projection. There are only two forces in the universe...love and fear. Only one of those forces is real. The other is an illusion. Love is extended by you; you who are love extended by God. When you extend love, you create reality. When you project, out of fear, you create illusion.

☺☺

A small and unique group of women who have been working on themselves spiritually and emotionally for a number of years gathered to experience "The We." After reminding them that they were all indeed magnificent multidimensional beings, "The We" invited them to participate in a journey of Self-discovery.

TRACY: I want to know what holds me bound to the house that I'm living in and what will set me free? And if it is financial, how can I be set free financially? What is it I need to learn and do?

HS: We understand and appreciate your question. We would like to lay a foundation for your understanding as together we look at this situation. We would remind you that you do create your reality. You do create your story. You do create the scenarios of your life. And you begin doing this at the very earliest stages of your physical existence.

To address directly the question of why you stay in the house you're in, we ask you to look at two dynamics. We understand that often in physicality you make your choice based on fear. We also understand you create your reality by extending love. We would suggest that everything you experience in your lifetime, from moment to moment, is an outward symbolic representation of an inner reality. If the inner reality is expressing in a fearful form or projecting outward from fear, it will create dynamics that may keep you busy and may keep life exciting or at least dramatic or suspenseful or action-packed, but not necessarily filled with peace, love, joy, and happiness.

So it is important to take a look at the fear that is causing you to stay where you are. We would ask you what thoughts come up when you think about the ideal situation in which you prefer to reside?

TRACY: I'd like to be in a house of my own with my two children.

HS: And when you think of that, what fear thought comes forth?

TRACY: Just now a thought of joy came forth, but when you were talking earlier I actually had a physical fear of going out on my own, like going out of the safety net of my home and going out on my own. I felt like there was bodily harm. I felt physically unsafe.

HS: We must remind you that the universe is a safe and abundant place; that your fears have all been created in your mind. They exist only in your mind. From your mind you project powerful dynamics that could create situations that limit you or frighten you or validate this thought you have, in your mind, that it's scary out there.

If you will choose love and remember who you are and reclaim your power as a co-creator, you will have the power to create exactly the scenario and environment you prefer. It is a matter of faith, determination and then, total trust that the universe will unfold as it should for you in perfect Divine order.

Sometimes you doubt that, because you have forgotten who you are. We would remind you that you are not the Creator of yourself. You are God's creation. You are a thought in the mind of God. You are created in God's image and likeness. God, being a creator, has created you—who are also a creator.

Therefore, you create everything else in your universe. You create everything in your reality. You create it with the same Divine plan by which God created you because you function in His image and likeness, like Him. The only thing you don't create is yourself. So give thanks to the Creator, God, All That Is, who created you. Recognize His will, to be done by you...under His plan as His creation. And then pursue the act of creating your extensions of God and yourself in the manner you desire for ultimate joy, peace, and happiness. Does this serve you?

TRACY: Yes it does.

MARYANNE: I have three questions and I think they're related because they all have to do with fears. One is about my relationship with my partner and what do I have to do not to ruin it because my fears usually get in the way? How can I help my daughter get rid of her fears because her fears sabotage her? And what can I give to my brother who is in more fear than I can even imagine?

HS: Would you be surprised to learn that the answer is the same for each of the questions you asked? The answer is love.

You are looking for the gift to give the people that you care about. The gift is always love.

MARYANN: But my love doesn't give them confidence.

HS: You can't give them confidence. You can only give them love. Confidence is something they will have to decide belongs to them. And they will decide that whenever they decide that—or not, but it won't have anything to do with you. They will be able to more easily love themselves, with confidence, when they are bathed in love. Love begets love. Fear motivates more fear. So your job is not to bring them anything, or give them anything, or do anything for them other than to share with them your love.

We would say that it is our sense that your heart's desire is to be a kind, loving and responsible person. We sense that you may not be clear on what responsibility is. We would remind you that taking responsibility means being able to respond. Being able to respond to the truth you know deep in your heart. That is true in your relationship with everyone in your life and it is especially true in your relationship with yourself. Your relationship with yourself will always be reflected back to you via your relationships with your loved ones...and your enemies.

You are love.

You all are loved by unseen forces that stand by each and every one of you to witness your experience and to support your experience and to assist your fulfilling of the growth of your spirit.

We would remind all of you who have spoken questions tonight and those of you who hold your questions in your thoughts but have yet to speak, that everything that happens in your physical experience is an opportunity for you to grow spiritually. The things that you struggle with the most are your biggest opportunities to experience tremendous spiritual growth.

Would you care to deal with the relationship with the man in your life in terms of trying to see it as an opportunity for spiritual growth? What area of difficulty seems beyond you right now?

MARYANNE: Actually it doesn't seem difficult right now. The only thing that I think would come between us would be if I give in to potential fears.

HS: Is the relationship good at this moment, right here, right now?

MARYANNE: Yes.

HS: Then that's all you need to know. It seems to us that perhaps you lost sight for a moment of the fact that the relationship is perfect here and now. And perhaps you jumped into the future and scared yourself with what might be. But we would remind you that in the present moment—and that is all there ever is, this Now Moment—you are safe.

Fear always lives in the future. When you are afraid, stop and remember that right now you are alive and you are breathing and you are safe. And the only way fear has any meaning to you is in a corner of your mind that has jumped into the future and worried about what might be. But it's all happening in your mind.

It's all right. It's just that human beings have not taken a great deal of time to recognize that reality is all happening in the mind. The illusion that it is happening in front of your eyes is such a powerful illusion that you think you are seeing something that unquestionably has reality.

Maybe your eyes aren't that trustworthy. Maybe you're not seeing what you think you're seeing.

We, the Voice of Spirit, have the advantage of having a perspective that is far less limited than the perspective that comes with physicality. So we offer you this gift by telling you that things aren't as they seem to be. And we ask you only to trust that may be so, from a perspective beyond what you're capable of perceiving in physicality.

As a persuasive argument to this point of view we would remind you that you are created in the image of God and not the other way around. God is not created in the image of man. God is a non-physical consciousness of such great proportion that to be limited simply to physicality is laughable.

You are also not limited to simple physicality. The part of you that is created in the image of God is limitless.

(Long pause.)

HS: We wish to ask that you simply accept the basic concept that you are more than your body. You are made of love and light. You have the opportunity in each Now Moment to choose love and extend yourself by extending love and creating as your Creator created you to create. You have a tendency to succumb to fear. In choosing that, you project your fear outward in a way that manifests a world of fear that you do not prefer and that does not bring you peace.

Our unconditional love to you.

MARYANNE: Thank you.

Facing Tragedy

Another recurring theme in the messages we've received over the years is the reminder to look for the blessing in even the worst of the worst. In this section we will share several sessions about facing tragedy, despair and numerous forms of bad news with insight and optimism.

Perhaps the most tragic was the violent car crash that claimed the lives of a young mother and her five children. Her husband, who had been a student of Denny's when she was a special education teacher years earlier, was the only one to survive this fiery crash.

DENNY: I'm here to ask you what my colleague and I can do therapeutically to help a young man we both know to cope with the tragedy of losing his entire family in a split second disaster.

HS: There is no end to the possibilities of good work that can be channeled by the two of you if you will open to Spirit and allow the work to take place. We would remind you that there is in the life of this young man, and all human beings, the understanding that every aspect of their experience is created for the journey of the Self to discover Itself and to realize Its connection to God. Every experience, every person, every thought, every deed carries with it the potential for this growth and Self-awareness.

The event that is called birth provides an opportunity for one to journey home to God. An experience called death is also an equal opportunity for Self realization and another step in your journey home.

Such is the case with this young man you have before you, one who has been given a huge opportunity to awaken. And it is our observation the measure of tapping on his consciousness was commensurate with his need to be awakened. It was necessary to his growth that he experience something of tremendous impact, for he was deeply asleep and heading down a road that took him nowhere in the fulfillment of his Divine blueprint for this lifetime.

The opportunity is in his face, so to speak, and we would observe that he is seizing the moment to expand his consciousness, extend his love, and grow to his highest spiritual potential. So if in your work with him you will focus on the positive aspects that lay before him for his growth and service to all mankind, rather than getting lost in the tragedy, pain and heartbreak of the form in which the lesson came—you will serve him in the most positive and beneficial way.

DENNY: It seems to me that the magnitude of the tragedy has to be processed first before anything can happen for him.

HS: We suggest that this is so. The pain remains so great at this point that the next step of unfoldment and spiritual development cannot occur as easily as it will once the tragedy is put to rest...or placed in its proper perspective. His good work will be distracted by the nightmare and visions of death by fire, so the Post Traumatic healing tool that you both know is not by accident. It provides for the perfect unfoldment of the Divine plan for you and for him, and for your colleague to work together in this miracle. And the process has the potential of performing the miracle. As you have been told in your study course, there is no degree of difficulty in miracles. The realization of the perfection of the Divine plan will allow the miracle to take place.

DENNY: I'm frightened at the prospect. It's a test of my own faith.

HS: We would remind you that it's not a test for you at all...for you are not charged with having to do the miracle. You are there to facilitate and witness the miracle that We shall provide.

DENNY: That helps.

HS: We would suggest you enter a meditative state before the work begins that allows you in whatever time it takes—and that could be a split second to a few moments—to be still and know in the depth of your being the truth... the truth that you have studied, the truth that you teach, the truth of which you lovingly remind each and everyone who enters your sanctuary. And once you have grounded yourself in the truth there will be no fear, for truth is love and love and fear cannot occupy the same space at the same time.

DENNY: Yes. Is it important that my colleague and I do this piece of work together?

HS: It is as much an opportunity for the two of you as it is for him. It is a perfect coming together of those who have gifts to give so that they may receive.

DENNY: I do trust that is so.

HS: By participating in giving him the gift of the miracle, you can receive the miracle as well.

DENNY: Yes. Thank you.

HS: If he is receptive to a new perspective that begins to recognize the gift he has been given in the opportunity to transform his life and serve the world, it may be of great comfort to him to know he journeys the rest of this life's path with the companionship of his wife and children who have not left. They have only changed form. They are not gone. And they are powerfully loving and giving Angelic guides ready to help him in completing his life task of love and service on this planet.

We feel this may be sufficient unto the time and we send you our unconditional love.

☺☺

In thinking back on her therapeutic session with that young man, Denny is touched by the recollection that it was a sacred moment.

"As we sat in the presence of this tragedy the room took on a glow—a glow of Spirit," she recalls. "It felt like being in the presence of an Enlightened Being. Grace and love surrounded him and it could be felt by all of us. It was a Holy Moment."

Fear of Pain

Nearly everyone who has talked with "The We" has harbored fear in one form or another. Often it is the fear of death. Sometimes it is fear of pain, as in this conversation with our friend Gemma.

GEMMA: When I see someone in a lot of pain, I understand that if they were to perceive their situation from a different perspective, they might not necessarily have that much pain or resistance, but they don't have access to that other perspective.

HS: You may be of assistance by helping them to consider another way of being or doing. But, you cannot force them to make a choice that you would prefer, or even force them to make a choice that in your perspective would ease their pain or improve their life. You can serve them with compassion by understanding that they will never create more pain for themselves than they can handle, including what you perceive as the ultimate pain...death.

The action they take, and the scenario they create, whether you can see it or not, will serve them. Sometimes it serves them by simply showing them a way in the future that they prefer not to go.

GEMMA: Do you mean in a future lifetime?

HS: Or even in this lifetime. It may seem inconceivable to you that in a given lifetime someone's so called unfortunate circumstance could be reversed, but the miraculous is possible if the belief system of the individual allows for change, remission, recovery, healing.

This is not a new concept, but because it is contrary to many people's long held beliefs and definitions of reality... they have difficulty applying it to day-to-day existence.

GEMMA: It's a compelling question for me because I have a lot of fear, not of death, but of pain.

HS: We have a sense that there was in a past lifetime some extreme pain in terms of physical discomfort that is still remembered in the cells of this current body, which after all was created by an essence that on one level of consciousness remembers all past lives. We would say to you once again, please dear one, don't be too hard on yourself.

You can respect and appreciate your feelings and need

not feel compelled to deny them or shut them off. It is better to embrace them, experience them, and let them flow through you as you allow the next new feeling to come forth that will be more representative of the direction you prefer to go.

DENNY: I have a question. If the belief is that we are somehow victims, then will the perception be that everyone who suffers from a physical or mental disability, or problem, or dysfunction...

HS: The people in your reality who look like they are having a difficult life are symbols of the false belief you still hold that says you are victims.

DENNY: And a way to help them heal is by healing our own inner wounds?

HS: That's why we continue to suggest that you recognize inner realities by viewing the physical symbols you find in your outer reality. They will serve as a clue to the area within that you would profit from learning to love. And love will be the transforming element that releases you from your victim-hood.

As you grow, your outer world symbols will change to reflect the new you. And you can indeed do away with starvation, war, deprivation and disease and all those symbols that represent your negative concepts.

The most helpful tool we could give you is "If it is not love...it is fear." Hold this dear to yourselves as you go through life.

Unconsciousness and Fear of Death

Earlier in this book we described an evening with a half

dozen friends in our Alamo home when "The We" managed to knock out the entire room. While listening to a discourse on dimensions of consciousness, everyone simply went unconscious. The next day Denny again consulted "The We" to ask for an explanation of what caused an entire group of people to go unconscious like that. Here's what we learned:

DENNY: I want to know why we got knocked out last night.

HS: We provided an opportunity earlier that evening that was designed to get all of you in touch with the fact that you are not your body. It came in response to a question that one member of the group asked about the impending transition of her father.

You are Existence that creates a physical body for a temporary period of time. In demonstrating to you that you are more than your body we mapped the areas of consciousness for you to experience...showing how your Existence manifests in different aspects of your own consciousness. We were able to facilitate your going to the core of your Being and experiencing Existence...pure Existence. While consciousness occurs in the mind, it does not include all the affiliated and associated expressions that mind presents in physicality, for example, memory.

When you have the experience of pure centered Self... Beingness...Existence...Essence, you are in an area that is without thought, without feeling, without belief systems, without knowingness. In pure existence there is no memory and so there are no words to describe it and no thoughts to recall it. In that state of pure existence you do literally go to a space that is void.

And that is what you did. You all went into the Void.

DENNY: Oh my.

HS: Now the purpose of that experience was to give you a first hand experiential demonstration of your continued Existence. None of you died in the process. None of you ceased to exist, as you are all back here now...perhaps with no memory or recall of what you experienced in that state. But you did experience pure Beingness and it is a very wholesome, nurturing, nourishing, creative, healthy experience that would serve you well to repeat on a regular basis.

DENNY: Like meditation?

HS: Yes.

DENNY: Okay. All that's fine, but there's something that really upsets me and that's the fact that I can't remember. Is there a way to cultivate the consciousness to go into the Void and bring back the memory?

HS: Why would you want to? Why would you want to complicate a pure experience of being with the clutter that accompanies thought? Or feeling? Or memory? Or words? As soon as you begin working or thinking or speaking words...you are doing. One cannot be doing and being.

DENNY: I understand that. It's just that afterwards it might be nice to be able to have recall, because it's a nice habit to be able to recall events. Being able to recall gives me a sense of continuity.

HS: You now can see another area in which you hold an attachment. You are attached to a definition of who you are.

DENNY: I am. And you know what really upsets me is the fact that I'm going to die and I'm not going to care who I was. This me, this Denny Reynolds that exists now won't matter.

HS: Well, given the truth of that situation we would urge you to thoroughly enjoy the Denny that exists now.

DENNY: There's such a desire to hold on to it. There really is. It's the biggest thing that upsets me the most about transition and dying...and that's that I won't be me anymore. I mean, I'll be me, but I won't be this me. I won't have these memories. I won't look at it through this perspective. And I guess that's why it becomes important to trust that there's something even better in store.

HS: We offer this experience and this information to enable you to fully appreciate the magnitude of yourself. We see no need to feel frustrated or depressed or anything but joyful over the absolute truth that you exist. You always have, you always will, regardless of what inability your physical mind and brain have to recall or define the experience of the existence of past lives or the recognition of future lives.

Preparing for a Loved One to Die

That gathering of friends in our home included a woman who was concerned about the ill health of her father. She asked how she could assist him in preparing for death.

MARY: I'd like to know...my father is ill. He may be getting ready for transition. Is there anything I can do to assist him?

HS: We would suggest that your love is the greatest gift you can give him or anyone. And we would assure you that in this time it will be helpful for you to understand that transition does not mean the end of existence. You exist. He exists. You all will always exist. You cannot not exist. You will only change form. So the transition will not be an end of his beingness. It will only be an end to this chapter of his existence in this physicality. He is a sovereign being who, like each and every one of you, will always create a reality that furthers his spiritual growth. Termination of physicality at this time is also a step toward his experiencing great spiritual growth and moving to higher realms of consciousness and experience.

To address your question as to how to be of service to him, understand that there is not one degree of negativity to the journey upon which he embarks. It is a grand continuance of the adventure that has been his life. Your love and expression of that love will enhance his journey and enable him to continue on this path of growth, knowing that you love, honor, and support him.

We would urge you to take time to be still and know. In being still and silencing the chatter of your mind and inviting Spirit to make its blessings apparent to you, you will receive guidance as to very specific things you can do in the coming days to present him with the kind of support that would be especially meaningful and helpful to him as he continues his journey.

VII

Reflections and Relationships

As we have mentioned before, a major piece of the teaching from "The We" revolves around the principle that everything is a symbolic reflection of an inner reality. Our life experiences always reflect what we think or feel, whether we're consciously aware of our inner attitudes or not.

DENNY: If everything in my physical reality is a reflection of beliefs from my inner reality, then is it also true that as I grow to accept and embrace the various pieces of myself, the clients who come to me will grow regardless of what I do? They will be reflections of my greater love and acceptance of myself.

HS: Yes. The clients who come to you are members of your holographic presentation. They will reflect and symbolize your relationship to concepts about yourself. And, it should not be taken as such a chore to work on this stuff, either focused on the dynamics of their lives or trying to figure out the inner reality of your life. Once again, we would suggest that your best choice is to stay focused on what seems real and honest in your heart, rather than trying too hard to figure out these client stories.

DENNY: Yes. With some people I really get sucked into their stories and with others I have no difficulty seeing the bigger picture.

HS: That often has to do with how the symbol has been processed or ignored in your own reality. The dynamics that have been addressed and satisfied in your personal consciousness are easier to work with in other people's lives.

DENNY: Yes, and the areas where I'm stuck present a bigger challenge. So, can I use your consciousness to explore my relationships with certain people that are troubling to me or areas that I haven't worked through?

HS: The question you have directed to us, we would direct to you. Ask yourself that question. Can you?

DENNY: Yes, I want to.

HS: Excellent.

DENNY: And what I want to do is look at one particular client and her entanglement and enmeshment in a way that I also have been. I'd like to get clarification as to why I often wind up in the middle of things, trying to control situations.

HS: The situation you describe is much like a tangled ball of string, tangled beyond repair so that it must be thrown away. The possible lesson in one's life when this occurs is a demonstration of not being true to one's basic inner belief. Each time you stray even a little bit off the path, you risk the possibility of getting your string tangled a little, so to speak. One often tends to go through life thinking a little tangle here and there won't matter much. You think you have no problem with these little matters until you find that your string is such a mess that you must now throw it away.

DENNY: Yes, it's all those little untruths.

HS: You have an opportunity to lead an impeccable life. It is a choice you make, step by step, in your journey. The choice is always, always between what you know to be the truth and the story you tell yourself. The pain you experience is the difference between the truth you know and the life you live.

Nature of Love

In July of 2004 we began a series of monthly Sunday night Spiritual Circles for interested people.

HS: We are here to remind you that each of you has a Voice Within that is available by invitation and it is as simple as remembering, as the Bible says, to "Be still and know." In that stillness, in that non-thinking quietness, in that still point lies the wisdom you seek. In stillness lies truth.

MALE: What is love?

HS: Love is what you are. Love is the basis of all that is. Love is the only reality. All else is illusion. Love has been extended by your Creator to create you in His image and likeness. That makes you loving beings of radiant light. That makes you creators that the Creator created. Your consciousness is powerful. And contrary to a long held belief which says because you were born into a body you have a mind which creates consciousness—contrary to that belief—the truth of the matter is your consciousness created your body and not the other way around.

Your consciousness is a powerful force in the universe, and that brings us back to your question, "What is love?" Love is that force—that consciousness that is who and what you are as an extension of the Creator, God, Goddess, All That Is. Is this helpful?

MALE: Yes.

Finding the Right Relationship

Having read this far you have become familiar with the idea that we create our own reality and we do it through our thoughts and beliefs. "The We" have frequently explained over the years that our physical reality is always a reflection of our inner reality. This was driven home when Denny asked about the possibility of a future relationship for our divorced older son. He has since found that loving relationship and Denny had the honor of officiating at a Spiritual Partnership ceremony for the two of them.

HS: There is always a probability for a primary relationship for any being when they come to an understanding that the person they are looking for is right in front of them. In other words, the idea of searching for an ideal mate is a false notion. The person you're searching for is right in front of you. Your relationship with yourself will be symbolized by the perfect person standing in front of you at the time that you accept who you are.

The basis of our teaching is best exemplified in this reminder: the relationships and physical objects in your life are all symbols of an inner reality. Your life is a teaching, with experiences being tools to help you understand your lessons. So, by taking a look at your physical surroundings you will come to an understanding of your inner truth.

Extramarital Relationships

A provocative question about man-woman relationships was asked by a female friend.

FEMALE: I have a question regarding marriage. If one of the married partners has a relationship with another man or woman outside the marriage, what is that?

HS: We see only relationship as being significant. We see that you in physicality, in your current society, have belief systems and rules and regulations that set up certain parameters for what is socially acceptable by consensus agreement.

We feel that one of your major growth experiences comes from re-evaluating the belief systems that are ruling your life and determining whether those beliefs continue to serve you. So when you ask about agreements between married couples and compare that to other existing relationships, we would ask that you remove all existing beliefs as to what is the appropriate social structure and look at what truly serves the individual in relationship to another individual. And the criteria for determining the success or failure of any relationship has to do with how that relationship furthers and nurtures the growth of the soul...the Spirit, regardless of what outside influences dictate should be recognized as appropriate behavior.

So, to cut to the chase...we would suggest you go within and determine what nurtures your being and not allow outside influences to dictate your behavior or experience. Is this of assistance to you?

FEMALE: Yes.

HS: We would simply remind you that all of your experiences in physicality are a result of your inner reality expressing itself in an unlimited form in your day-to-day physical experience. And it all comes from within—and when you have a struggle or difficulty interpreting or understanding what appears to be "out there" coming at you, you're best served by remembering that it originates "within you" and always reflects the internal processing that is going on within you to find balance, harmony, wholeness and completion. And to do that there are often experiences that seem sometimes to be difficult or to involve struggle. But never are they beyond what you are capable of dealing with or beyond what is presented by yourself to yourself as a great gift...a great opportunity to discover and integrate, understand and appreciate another aspect of yourself.

No person can manifest in your life without having been generated through you as a symbolic representation of some aspect of you. You are the center of your universe. You are the creator of your universe. You are the totality of your universe. There is *nothing* outside of you. All that which appears to exist outside of you is a product of your consciousness. Your consciousness creates every aspect of your reality from the clothes you wear to the mates you choose to the stars you see at night and the planets in the universe. *All* of your reality is self-generated. *Everything.*

FEMALE: So if I look outside myself whatever I see is a reflection of inside and if I see beauty it's a reflection and if I see ugly it's a reflection?

HS: Yes.

FEMALE: And we do have a choice in it?

HS: Yes. You are all of it. You are *all* of it. You forget from moment to moment and thereby experience what you perceive as difficulty or uncomfortableness, despair, discomfort, or joy and happiness. All ends of the spectrum, you are responsible for. They all originate within *you.*

FEMALE: When you say *"you"* are you speaking of all of us?

HS: We speak to you who have inquired and we understand that you are all that exists in your universe. The channel also exists, but he is all that exists in his universe, of which you have agreed to be a part. And in your universe, he has agreed to be a part, and in her universe you both have agreed to be a part. And she has agreed to be part of yours—but you are totally unique and individual universes. Totally unique and distinct and creating every aspect of that part of your unique individual universe. And in your agreement to co-create, you find similarities that allow you to exist together in this Now Moment to share this experience. You also all simultaneously exist in multidimensional experiences of which you are not now aware because your focus is here. But you are grand multidimensional beings who exist on many levels in many places simultaneously and function with absolute impeccability in each of these other experiences of which you have no notion here and now, for your focus puts in your awareness only this "Now" reality.

Feeling Disappointed with a Friend

There is a line in the *Desiderata* (written by Max Ehrmann in 1927) which says, "... whether or not it is clear to you, no doubt the universe is unfolding as it should." This has been reiterated time and again by "The We" to the point that Denny and I have reconditioned our thinking and trained our minds constantly to look for the blessing in the most challenging events of our lives. We were inspired by this session from September of 1999.

HS: We are here.

DENNY: We'd like any insights you can share on our experience of being disappointed by the way certain things turn out. Most recently a friend failed to make it to one of our workshops. It seems like you can't count on things. I don't know what that means, so if you have anything to share on the subject I would appreciate it.

HS: We would share a few words about disappointment. The lesson that is available to you in noticing your disappointment is again having a higher view of your life rather than getting caught in your story. A higher view of life understands that disappointment is merely your getting trapped in your notion of how something should occur and loosing sight of the perfection of it all. Either the universe unfolds as it should one hundred percent of the time—or it doesn't. We can tell you when you feel it doesn't, that is only a misperception on your part. It is your inability or lack of faith that says what is happening now is less than perfect. It is all perfect. It is all one hundred percent perfect, one hundred percent of the time. You will sometimes be aware of this and you will sometimes forget this, but the principle remains constant—the universe truly unfolds as it should... in Divine perfection one hundred percent of the time.

DENNY: Does that mean that life is just a process of allowing whatever is there, to be there? Because that doesn't always work for me. Sometimes it's incredibly painful.

HS: Life is always an opportunity to grow spiritually. "Allowing" is a very healthy way to experience your life and grow spiritually. You are in a "free-will universe," so you can always make whatever choice you wish, and you can always position yourself in relationship to the events of your life in any manner you wish. You can bring whatever grand amount of consciousness to that choice, judgment or relationship. Or you can bring only a limited amount of consciousness to that choice. It is all up to you. From our perspective the higher vibrational forms of consciousness produce more joy, balance, harmony, and ease of existence than those lower vibrational choices that include effort, struggle, agony, and pain.

DENNY: Well for me this is a matter of trust. Is it possible to trust another human being to be what they say they are and do what they say they'll do?

HS: The answer to that has to do with the amount of trust contained within you for the individuals in your life. Every single relationship you experience will be a reflection of the relationship you have with yourself...on whatever subject is being focused upon at any given time.

DENNY: So this friend who didn't show up at our workshop was a reflection of my letting myself down?

HS: Your feelings about that, yes.

DENNY: You mean at anytime I can just dump my inner child and go off and....

HS: Haven't you?

DENNY: Yes, I guess I have. Oh boy! And I'm still struggling. That's a painful reflection, the reflection of dumping myself. I just don't know what to do. I just don't know how to feel. I don't like this reflection.

HS: Would you appreciate our perspective? As we see it you have a choice here to grow spiritually or stagnate in self-indulgence. We see this as an opportunity for you to let go of willfulness and old habits and your past ways of doing things that have not allowed you to move forward in joy and harmony. Again, you live in a free will universe. You can choose to relate to this situation from whatever level you desire and we would ask you to ask yourself, which choice serves my Higher Self in the highest manner?

DENNY: I guess I can't make it be any different than it is. I can rail against it and that changes nothing. And I can get angry and that changes nothing. I'm disappointed because I just wanted...

HS: (Interrupting) You have left out a huge possible choice. What do you suppose would happen if you embrace the perfection of your experience at this time and place?

DENNY: I don't even know what that means.

HS: Instead of finding fault with it or feeling hurt by it or feeling victimized by it or feeling frustrated by it or feeling a lack of understanding of it...why not expand large enough to embrace it as a perfect experience in this time and place for your spiritual growth? Even if you can't describe the benefits of it, allow that it is so and ask for some understanding.

DENNY: Okay. What I'm getting right now is about learning not to count on anyone in the old way that I used to. It's different somehow. I'm not sure how to count on people, but I'm really getting the feeling that I'm alone in this world.

HS: Well, it's not a matter of "not counting on people." It's a matter of counting on people to function appropriately and in Divine perfection one hundred percent of the time. It's not that anyone has done anything inappropriate to your spiritual growth. Your friend has played her role perfectly; otherwise you wouldn't have this opportunity right now to come to a greater understanding of who you are.

DENNY: It's like not needing anybody to be a certain way for me to feel good about myself. That's the lesson for me.

HS: It's more than that. It's not just "not needing them to be," it's understanding that they are being perfect. You still have a judgment that somebody let you down or did something wrong or didn't follow the right script...

DENNY: That's right.

HS: What movie are you in for heaven's sake?

DENNY: Mine. My movie. And they're supposed to do it my way. (Laughter.) And I don't like it when they don't.

HS: We don't mean to scold you, for we love you unconditionally, but sometimes we think you're stubborn.

DENNY: (Laughing.) That's what all day yesterday was about. It was about me wanting it my way and it's not going my way. Oh God, I think this is what I'm learning. My little ego's just hanging on for dear life...demanding. I feel like a little kid. A disappointed little child.

HS: Would it help to stamp your feet?

DENNY: Maybe.

HS: Then we encourage to you to stamp your feet.

DENNY: Well maybe I just will.

HS: Would it help to beat on a pillow? Then we encourage you to beat on a pillow.

DENNY: I just feel sad.

HS: Then we encourage you to feel being sad.

DENNY: I guess life will be what it is and my goal for this year....

HS: Well once you get finished feeling really sad, then you can choose to feel really happy or somewhere in between. You will finish with feeling sad eventually. It cannot go on indefinitely.

DENNY: This is just the hardest work—to let go...To trust that there's a bigger plan; that this is just a story in my head.

HS: And so, this is sufficient to the time. We wrap our essence around your essence and send you joy and light and love and happiness, which will remain available to you until the time you choose to embrace and experience those gifts from us.

Speaking One's Opinion

Did you ever have an uneasy situation with a friend? It's

someone you obviously care about and have a significant relationship with, but every now and then the relationship just doesn't seem to work. You know it's not right, but you're not sure what's wrong. Such an encounter with a friend led Denny to a very revealing conversation with "The We."

DENNY: I had an encounter with a friend yesterday that left me feeling physically ill. I just don't feel good about it and I don't know where to look for help.

HS: We will help you explore the dynamics of this relationship. Let us take a look at the most prevalent feeling first. What would you say that is?

DENNY: I feel angry and hurt.

HS: First let's look at the hurt. Perhaps you would appreciate some clarification as to what the experience means?

DENNY: Yes.

HS: The experience of feeling hurt is a dramatization of an inner fear. In your inner reality a false belief exists on a very deep, unconscious level that you are unworthy. We would like to remind you that situations occur in your life to give you an opportunity to test feelings you have about yourself. These situations are opportunities to overcome feelings of unworthiness, to develop esteem and pride in your very nature. The encounter with your friend can be seen as an opportunity to stand tall in the face of challenge, to learn that you do not have to give yourself up.

DENNY: That's exactly how I feel.

HS: So the situation we have now is one of feeling hurt when you look back on your encounter because your friend challenged you and you responded by doubting your "knowingness." So the hurt you feel is a self-inflicted wound. While it appears to have come from your friend, it is really a sadness you feel for having let yourself down.

DENNY: I'm aware that I edited and censored myself so much yesterday that I tolerated the intolerable.

HS: We would observe that you did not take very good care of yourself. We would also lovingly observe that there is perhaps some confusion on your part about trying to be nonjudgmental, and therefore not standing up for yourself. It is not unloving to take good care of yourself and to demonstrate self-esteem. In this attempt to be nonjudgmental, you not only betrayed yourself—but you also did not accomplish "nonjudgmentalness."

DENNY: No, I did not.

HS: Your judgments were abundant.

DENNY: (Laughing.) Yes, and more so than usual.

HS: So what you have here is a grand opportunity to take a look at what you experienced and to focus on what your role was in this situation and to explore another way of being. It is true that "guilt is merely a lesson unlearned." You now have the choice to either feel guilty about yesterday's performance or...

DENNY: (Interrupting.) Performance?

HS: Yes. All of life is a play. So you may critique yesterday's performance and feel guilty, or you may rejoice in seeing that yesterday's performance provided an opportunity to do things differently in the future. Does this help you?

DENNY: Absolutely. In looking at my performance yesterday I see all those things I didn't say to my friend.

HS: May we make an observation?

DENNY: Yes.

HS: We would suggest that some of the things you did not say were censored in an attempt not "to be cruel." We would suggest that you may take a further step in the future, when that happens again, to ask yourself, "What is the most loving way now to express what I am withholding?" There will come to mind the perfect words to use lovingly to serve your friend and yourself as well.

DENNY: Yes. I was also worried the whole time that if I said anything I could not only offend my friend, but my husband would also be furious.

HS: And your assessment of that precarious situation was absolutely correct. What we are suggesting will keep you out of trouble with him as well. In other words, ask the question, "How can I most lovingly serve my friend with my honest reaction to this situation?"

You will find a way of neutralizing the situation that will have your friend's gratitude and your husband's blessing. It will simply be another opportunity to speak Truth. Don't get caught in side excursions. Don't get drawn off track. There is no competition. There is no game that needs to be won. Remember, Truth and Love are synonymous.

DENNY: At least I was aware enough yesterday to stop long enough to have a little chat with myself about the situation as it was happening.

I said to myself, "Pay attention. You're censoring everything. Stop and pay attention. Just detach and notice where you are and maybe later you can figure out what's going on."

HS: We compliment you on your awareness and we are trying to give you an additional piece of information that will take you one step beyond where you finished yesterday.

DENNY: I did get stuck yesterday. I became afraid that I'd be drawn into it without consciousness and that I would just be reacting.

HS: Future situations can be likened to the experience that is underway at this moment. We are using the channel's consciousness, vocabulary and knowledge to transmit information that he would not sit down and consciously create. He is literally acting as a channel. You can also literally become a channel in future encounters with your friend. Channel your Higher Self. When you do, you will speak the truth in the most loving manner.

DENNY: Of course I will. I do that all the time in my work.

HS: This is an even greater challenge than in your work situations. Mastering this challenge with your friend will provide some of your greatest growth.

We have looked at the feeling of hurt. Would you now like to explore your anger? We would encourage you to speak about your anger.

DENNY: I felt "not valued." I felt invisible.

HS: Do you see again how this symbolizes an inner reality where it seems you have something to prove? And the truth of the matter is you have to prove nothing. Your magnificence, your knowledge, your wisdom, your experiences do not have to be defended.

DENNY: The relationship often feels competitive.

HS: That is because of your own doubt...of your worthiness and your wisdom.

DENNY: My mother used to compare me on a regular basis with other people to assess how I was.

HS: We would remind you that your mother's comparisons were simply another symbolic expression of your inner reality—your own inner doubting of your worthiness. We are suggesting that when you recognize your worthiness, the symbols of doubt and comparison will disappear from your reality...from your experience.

So the experience with your friend is a re-enactment, so to speak, of your experience with your mother. But even that was just another symbolic representation of your own doubt about yourself, your lack of self-esteem. You simply have not recognized your own magnificence.

You have our permission—indeed you have our encouragement—and you serve the world when you recognize your own magnificence.

DENNY: I do know that, both intellectually and emotionally, but I have my blind spots and my friend is very good at flushing those out.

HS: We again commend you for being willing to feel the feelings and being willing to look at the symbols. We commend you for having the consciousness not to sweep this under the rug. We congratulate you for being willing to take it out into the light—to look at it and to learn from it.

DENNY: Sometimes I get confused and right now I feel stirred up because, in addition to this event with my friend, I had a recent spiritual conversation with another dear friend about looking at the bigger picture and moving into a conscious awareness of maya or the illusion of life. So, as I said, I feel stirred up.

HS: We are pleased. And we say this because when you are stirred up you are stimulated to have thoughts and feelings and experiences that bring you into a greater knowing of yourself. That is the purpose of life—to come to know and love every aspect of who you are.

We would suggest that you be easier on yourself. Do not struggle as much with the material. Allow it just to wash over you. You are learning on levels that you're not even aware of. You are learning how the universe works and what your part is in it.

DENNY: I'm also in touch with a difficult telephone conversation I had with a friend. If everything is an outward symbol of an inner reality, the unpleasant conversation must be symbolic of my own inner reality and yet I don't know how to trace that back—to find it.

HS: This is as much a symbol of your inner reality as the other things in your life that we have already discussed, and in this situation you have an opportunity to learn not to judge yourself so harshly. The expressions of negativity for which you have judged your friend are opportunities for you to be a little more loving and accepting of yourself through a loving acceptance of her. Now, that is not to suggest that you have to act in an arrogant manner, just because she has, but you can embrace the arrogance and have an understanding of what it symbolizes. In this case there are symbols within symbols to be considered. Your friend's arrogance, that you find abhorrent, is merely symbolic of her fear of not being good enough.

While it is easy to see it when it exists in your friend, it is more difficult to see it in yourself. In yourself perhaps it does not manifest in the flamboyant manner your friend exhibits, but nonetheless it is an aspect of your personality as well...and one that has not been fully accepted by you.

DENNY: Well, all I know is I'm reacting so fast that I can't seem to catch myself.

HS: Perhaps you could use your awareness of the experience as if it were a "reset button." Use the situation to say, "Opps—buzzer, buzzer. There's something here for me to take a look at and to learn to love."

If you can learn that the little girl that dwells within your friend is hiding beneath the bigger-than-life version of herself when she laughs her arrogant laugh; and instead of seeing that arrogant, flamboyant being, if you can see the little frightened child it will help you remember that within you is also a little frightened child. And, both children need love.

Other People's Decisions

As a psychotherapist, Denny has learned that if you do it one place, you do it everywhere. In other words, if you exhibit a certain style of behavior in one relationship you will find yourself behaving that way in all of your relationships.

DENNY: I've noticed that along with the stuff concerning my friend, I am also closing down around my youngest son and experiencing constriction.

HS: That is the insidious nature of fear. It doesn't just close down around one relationship or one concept. It closes down around the entire being and every expression of your being.

DENNY: I'd like to talk more about my son.

HS: Very well. We would remind you that you may choose to worry about him or not, that is your business. You may be as involved in his story as you wish. He will create the situations he needs to mature and grow and learn.

DENNY: Sometimes it's difficult to give up the old reality and move into a place of trusting.

HS: We would observe that you are saying on one hand that it's difficult to trust and on the other hand it is clear that you are choosing to trust in a negative reality.

DENNY: Okay. Is there anything I can do to aid my son in his own unfolding?

HS: You will best serve him through your enthusiasm for the way his life unfolds. So you have your answer to the question "What will I give?" Give love and comfort and compassion, coupled with the freedom that he needs to make his own choices. Both you and your husband have an opportunity in this experience with your son to come to better recognize the voice of fear—versus the voice of Love.

We would suggest that often you get caught because you feel compelled to listen to what you call "the voice of common sense." We would suggest that common sense often is biased toward the conventional fears that have been perpetuated in your society. So common sense will grasp the fear of not having enough money, or not doing a good enough job and so forth. Part of your growth experience will be finding the real voice that is common sense and recognizing what is the voice of fear.

DENNY: That's a struggle. Often times, as you said, the voice of common sense...

HS:...perpetuates the myth.

DENNY: Yes. It's just another form that fear takes to convince us that we have to do things according to rules that are external rather than internal.

HS: Yes. For example, your husband might do well to consider that if your son takes a six-day climbing trip, instead of working and bringing in a paycheck, that will be exactly the right experience. We can't tell you which choice is better, but we can tell you he cannot make a mistake. If he goes on the trip and some new adventure or avenue of opportunity opens up...that will be wonderful. And there is always the possibility for that unlimited potential. If he goes on the trip and does not acquire good fortune and a positive experience, but instead learns that he can't exist without six days' pay...he will have gained a new and wise piece of information and experience.

DENNY: And if he stays and does not go on the trip he has the same opportunities presented to him either to feel stifled and unable to produce, or...

HS: So this is an opportunity for him to learn to trust his heart... as is the case with all choices all people make.

We simply remind you that the decisions your son makes in this climbing opportunity will be influenced by his belief system. Your husband's observations of your son's experience will be influenced by his belief system. So we say to you if you hold on to a belief system that says you must continue to work and have six days' pay and that you cannot take six days leave because you will suffer financially—then if you hold on to that belief new opportunities will not come forth.

We would sum up by encouraging you and your husband

and your son to slow down the chatter in your minds, get out of your heads, feel from your hearts and then make your choice.

It is as much of a creation in your sovereign universe as it is in your husband's sovereign universe, as it is in your son's sovereign reality and you will co-create the final eventuality.

DENNY: I really feel in tune once again with the world of unlimited possibilities instead of with a world of limitation, fear and doubt.

Helping Others

Denny and I have often been reminded of the basic goodness of others when we hear people ask, with the utmost kindness and sincerity, how they can help their fellow man or improve their own behavior. "The We" have had some very interesting things to say over the years on the subject of helping others.

FEMALE: Is it ever possible to help anyone?

HS: You can always assist fellow beings by expressing your unconditional love for them. You can support one another through loving fellowship. You cannot take one's life assignment and complete it for them. You cannot lift anyone's load. You cannot intervene with anyone's higher, Divine blueprint and purpose. You can align yourself with the completion of their tasks and assignments with your loving understanding and support and with your unconditional love. You cannot perform another's task in any manner, shape, or form.

FEMALE: Unconditional love—does that include speaking our viewpoint?

HS: Truth and love are synonymous. You always assist another by sharing your loving truth. You never assist another by taking over any aspect of their life experience. We would remind you that whatever you do that takes away from someone else's opportunity to work through their challenges and have their spiritual growth does not serve them and does not serve you...and there will be consequences for such actions. So our best suggestion is remember that unconditional love is the greatest gift.

FEMALE: How will I know if it's coming from unconditional love?

HS: You will be able to know by stopping and asking for guidance and then being impeccable in your actions and decisions. We would suggest before you take any action, take several deep breaths, count to ten and see if this action serves you or serves them. Often humans step in to do what makes them feel better without recognizing what is in the best interests of the other. So we would counsel you to slow down, ask for guidance, open your heart, restate your determination to be of loving assistance unconditionally, and ask that Thy Will be done.

It is possible for each of you to become conscious of your Divine blueprint and the Divine blueprint of all those other beings with whom you are in relationship. It seems to us from the questions you have asked, that you would desire to be one who honors the other's Divine blueprint rather than imposing your own agenda on their lives. So if you state the intention to honor their Divine blueprint it will be apparent to you what is the best course to pursue and what is best not to embark upon. And remember, as we said earlier, you are the center of your universe and all these other relationships are merely symbolic representations of aspects of yourself. So, as you honor the blueprints of the people you are in relationship with, you are validating and allowing for the spiritual growth of aspects of yourself. The service is Divine. It serves those you're in relationship with as symbolic representation of aspects of yourself. So you have served your Self by dealing with them "out there."

All the aspects of your reality and life experience exist for the completion of your beingness. The more profound circumstances are often represented by close and immediate members of your family. The people closest to you represent the most significant inner aspects of yourself that are looking for completion, harmony, balance, wholeness, resolution. So when you have a child who causes you anxiety and grief and sorrow or concern or pain, that is the closest symbolic representation of that yet to be completed, accepted and loved aspect of your own self.

◎◎

In another session "The We" provided more insight on the power of love in service to others.

HS: We are here. How may we be of service to you?

FAYE: I have a question. How can I serve the people I love?

HS: It may appear that different answers apply to different situations and different people when one considers how to serve those you love. The answer is quite simple and uncomplicated and similar in every instance.

The answer is love.

So if you would like to assist someone, you may do so by reminding them that of everything they have accomplished and created...the one thing that remains outside of themselves is the fact they did not create themselves. They owe their existence to a Source outside themselves. There is much you can take responsibility for having created. In fact, all that you experience you have created—except you did not create yourself.

That which created you, is beholden to your existence. That which created you will guarantee your survival and continued existence. So the idea that you have something to fear is a total misperception. It is an illusion. It is not so. You can be fearful if you choose, but it has no foundation. It has no reality. Your Creator not only created you, but also maintains your existence and provides you absolute safety and security. If you understand this to the core of your being you will find ways to give this depth of understanding to those you love.

To answer your question as to how you can serve those you love, this is the path. This is the way. This is the truth. This is the light.

Is this of assistance?

FAYE: Yes. Thank you. I have another question. It's about group consciousness. Is it beneficial to the consciousness as a whole for a group of people to congregate and to be living in close proximity? Is it helpful to each of the individuals and to the consciousness as a whole?

HS: There is only one. There is no separateness. The idea

that you come together in a group of separate individuals is part of the illusion.

DENNY: You are the group? It's like there is only one Son of God and mankind is it.

HS: You come together in a realization that you are one and that is good work, as opposed to continuing to experience your physicality as separate, unattached people. There is one mind...one consciousness...one shared beingness, because you did not create yourself. You are a thought of God. God's mind exists in each and everyone one of you as one mind. So your individual experience of it and her individual experience of it is the experience of the "one mind" of God to which you are both connected. It's the same mind.

(Long pause.)

You are each sovereign individuals, but that does not negate the collected consciousness that binds you with your brothers and binds you with the Source that has created you. The interconnectedness gets more complicated. If you would like to know more we will share with you that your Creator created the person next to you and you also created the person next to you. And the person next to you created you. And your Creator created both of you. It gets a bit sticky and complicated, but it all hooks up if you can follow it to its highest point.

DENNY: It's the new perspective.

HS: For us it is a very old perspective.

Now, as to the friend you're concerned about, we would like to remind you that as much as you all are concerned for her wellbeing—and this is good work—we would remind you that only she creates her reality. You may not have any impact on her choices other than to exemplify the choice for love. You can exhibit that manifestation for her, but she must make the choice for love, rather than succumbing to the voice of fear.

FAYE: Is there a way I can remind her of that?

HS: Reminder is helpful. Example is even better. You might share with her your choice process. You might share with her how you determine which voice you listen to. You might share with her why you choose to have Holy Spirit be your teacher rather than the fear found in the voice of the ego. You might share with her the experiences of your life that have been blessed by having Holy Spirit occupy your mind versus the dilemmas that have been experienced in your life with the fearful voice of ego occupying your mind.

DENNY: This is so perfect. The book you're writing is a book of your life stories and didn't your friend just volunteer to type it for you? Oh that is so perfect.

HS: The universe unfolds as it should one hundred percent of the time and the work that has been set in motion here has great possibilities for healing. We would remind you that part of your friend's problem is preoccupation with and focus on the voice of fear. If you can divert her attention in a very simple way to something healthier without making a big deal out of it, there will be a shift in perspective. And it will happen before she even realizes what has happened to her. So have a good time. Enjoy her company. Allow her to make that journey with you toward your fulfillment, since she knows not how to pursue her own fulfillment. If she can accompany you on the wholesome journey of your fulfillment, she can benefit equally with you in the process.

Do what excites you the most. If you're willing to have her be a companion on your journey doing what excites you the most, she can heal in the process.

VIII

Work and Accomplishment

It has been very beneficial for us to apply the spiritual principles put forth by "The We" to every aspect of our lives. We've seen through experience that truth is truth and applies not only to what we'd ordinarily consider our spiritual life but also to the everyday experience of working for a living. These principles apply in every circumstance, one hundred percent of the time.

Being versus Doing

I will be the first to admit this relationship with "The We" has often felt like something in the realm of science fiction. In a strange way, that often gave more credibility to the thought that these words were coming *through me* and not *from me*. I would never say many of these things. In fact, at times I simply did not believe what was being said.

HS: What we have to say now is especially important, so we want you to pay particular attention. The word for today is "allow." Quiet your mind. Allow, allow...get out of the way. Now is the time to accept that these truths are so, and that the way of the world is such that one need not trouble one's mind with "figuring."

Things are what they are, whether you have figured them out or not. The world is not at all what you think it is. Existence is not at all what you think it is. The picture you have of reality is a tidy one, but totally contrary to what really is. In actuality, your environment is much safer than you have ever imagined and it is nothing like the picture you currently have of the universe.

You are totally safe and secure. In truth you have no enemies, no obstacles, no menaces. The challenges, threats, obstacles, fears, terrors that come your way are all created by you for your own self-involvement...or should we say evolvement. The forces of existence that lie before you are simply serene and uneventful. It is a blank slate. You give this blank canvas what you need to get. You are the painter, the painting, and the patron that views the art.

So make it whatever you want it to be. Paint. Enjoy. Behold. Do. See. Receive.

Career Direction

In conversations with dozens of people who have queried "The We" about various aspects of their lives, the message has been clear and consistent. You are not a victim. You always have choices. You are always free to choose again if your first choice doesn't pan out.

LINDA: I'm just going to have to talk and hopefully out of that you'll get some questions.

Well, one question is why am I overeating all the time? I'm getting fatter and fatter than I've ever been in my life.

The other question is more difficult for me to ask. I know there are many things in my life that are changing, always changing, but I know that in terms of my career there will be some major changes forced upon me.

HS: We do not believe that you are a victim. We do not see that change is ever forced upon you. We see that the experience of life is a series of choices and life flows from you and does not come at you.

LINDA: Okay. I understand that. So there are changes that are going to occur and I have choices...

HS: There are changes you are going to create and you have choices as to how you react to those situations.

LINDA: Right. The question is...I'm not sure what the question is. I want to do something different with my life, my career. I have always sensed...

HS: Do you have the picture clearly in your mind as to what you want to do?

LINDA: No.

HS: Then how is the universe going to give you what you want if you don't know and aren't clear as to what it is? You have great power. More than you can conceive. You have the assistance of unseen forces in helping manifest the perfect creation of your dream. But...you have to dream it.

LINDA: How do I get there?

HS: Decide what you want. Do what excites you the most. Have a picture. Feel the feeling.

You create your reality one hundred percent of the time anyhow. It's not that you have to learn how to do it. You do it. You're doing it right now. The life you have right now is one hundred percent a result of the thoughts and the feelings of previous Now Moments. And the thoughts and feelings that you have in this Now Moment will create the experience you have in the next Now Moment. And the more clear you can be on what you want, the more intention you can create, the more feeling you can feel about that creation the more it will manifest in the manner you prefer.

Do you not have an experience in this lifetime that is an example for you to sense the truth of what we have just said?

LINDA: I know that it's true. Yes, I have had. Boy, have I ever.

HS: Where is the doubt?

LINDA: The doubt is in that I don't know. That I know pieces...but not the...

HS: (Interrupting.) Fear is a very powerful force.

LINDA:...I haven't put a picture to it...

HS: (Interrupting again.) Fear stops creation or alters creation. Or you create and then, not realizing you have been afraid, you find yourself in situations not desirable and wonder how you got there—having forgotten the fear that was projected out to make that situation manifest.

We would remind you that more powerful than fear— the force in this universe that is undoubtedly more powerful than fear—is love. Extend love. Be love. Create your dream scenario with love. Love creating what you would love. Love loving the creation you've created. Love all the creations you've already created. Decide the creations you would love to experience in the future.

Love is the best antidote to fear. Denial is absolutely ineffectual with fear. Things you resist will persist. When you find fear thoughts occupying your mind, know that there are two things coexisting in your mind simultaneously. Know that you have two voices within you. You have two teachers available. One is the ego, occupying a portion of your mind, and it will always frighten you. The other is this Voice of Spirit that also occupies your mind and is love and can be chosen at any time. And It will be your ally and It has more power than the ego could ever have, because the ego has no power.

Fear is an illusion. Fear is not real. The power it seems to have you have given it. So our suggestion would be to say, "Fear is here." Embrace it. Don't resist it. Know that it is an opportunity for you to know something about yourself: the thing that you are afraid of is an opportunity to strengthen your character—to permit yourself to experience growth in a spiritual way. Know that you are the creator of your universe. You have created everything in your universe including the fear that frightens you at the moment. And know that when you come back to this Now Moment, you are here, you are safe. Pull yourself together and know that just as much as you let fear exist in the future you can let love exist in the future and you will create that future from the decisions you make, the thoughts you think, the beliefs you have in this Now Moment.

You are surrounded by unseen forces who love and support you always...in all ways.

The most helpful message we can give you at this point

is remember you are a thought in the mind of God and you are an extension of the Creator. You are protected by the Creator and are given freedom of choice by the Creator. So enjoy the wonderful, unlimited creative process and power that is within you to envision the ideal scenario for your total love and happiness and abundance and joy. We again send you our unconditional love and we would wrap our arms around you, if we had arms.

SANDY: I really don't have a question, but I've been listening to everything that you've been saying and I have such a strong sense of "doing that"—doing so many of those things—and of course that always makes me cry...

HS: We are so pleased to see that you all have such feelings. The tears you shed are a sign of an open heart. If you had instead shielded yourself from feelings what a shame that would be to cut off the important experience of the open heart.

We welcome you. What would you wish to express?

SANDY: I've listened to all the responses to everyone who has asked a question. The process that you give to them, that deals with their fear—overcoming fear and for facing their doubt. I've done that so much and I know what that is...

HS: And?

SANDY: And I wish I could give it to everybody. But it takes work. You have to do the work. Trust.

HS: And so you extend your love. And others who are able to receive it, do. And those who don't we have great compassion for and are dedicated to working with in whatever timetable is appropriate for their awakening. Enlightenment cannot be rushed. Enlightenment is an allowance that unfolds at its pace. And each and every one of you assists your brothers and sisters by allowing for their sovereignty—giving them companionship, compassion, and encouragement. Allowing them to unfold at their pace.

SANDY: I believe that. I give that to my children and I give it to my grandchildren.

HS: And this is good work. Our unconditional love to you.

How may we further serve you?

LUPE: I have pictures of things I wish to do and I'm trying to reach them. I try to go above the fears and I know I'm not strong enough.

HS: You do not need to be stronger. You need only to recognize the strength you already have. God gave you strength. God didn't take it away from you after He gave it to you. You lost sight of your strength perhaps, but that didn't diminish the fact that you are strong. You are powerful. You are a creator. Whether you recognize it or not has no bearing on the fact that it is so. You are strong. You do create.

So you may forget, but that doesn't take away or diminish your strength. And we have no condemnation of you for having forgotten. We exist to help you remember. We exist to help you awaken. We exist as the support team that helps you remember who you are, what your strength is. What your power is. What your purpose is. We are the Voice of Spirit. We are the Holy Voice of Spirit. We are here to remind you that our assistance is your birthright. Our assistance is your right prior to birth and after death. We exist to accompany you through eternity.

We remind you that you are love and your experience of fear is simply coming from having forgotten who you are. And that's all right. In the process you will be strengthened. In the process you will become aware of your beauty and your strength and your power. We will assist you. We are available for support and love and companionship and truth and love and light.

Worries about Money

A very good friend of ours is Dr. Sharon J. Wesch, although at the time we first met her name was Sher Wendt. She is a spiritual teacher, writer, and healer and she asked to have a session with "The We" hoping to gain insight on her current circumstances and future goals. Much of what she was told may be helpful to others and is used here with Sher's permission.

HS: We are here and we welcome this opportunity to assist you in any way we can. How may we serve you?

SHER: What I want to know is should I keep planning to put together a foundation? Is that going to unfold, or is that just a hope on my part?

HS: We would lay down some fundamental ideas that are merely a reminder of things you already know but may forget from time to time as you place your focus on the ever-popular human characteristic of "problem solving." And from our point of view problem solving is simply a little game you play to...

(Pause.)

SHER and HS: (Simultaneously)...amuse yourselves.

SHER: I knew that's what you were going to say.

HS: Now, as to what you can plan on or count on or depend on...the answer is *yourself*. You are living in a designer universe and *you* are the designer. It's not a question of what can you depend on having in the next Now Moment and the next Now Moment, but deciding what you want to create in the next Now Moment and the next Now Moment.

SHER: And I'm wondering why everything's shutting down as far as my work in California goes. Is there a message that I'm supposed to stop my work in California?

HS: The message that the universe gives you and all people is that you are loved...unconditionally. You are supported by unseen powers in the universe and all is well and all is safe. You can have anything you desire. The amount of doubt that you have about any particular part of your life will also manifest what may appear to be obstructions to your having your heart's desire. Your doubt will manifest roadblocks to what you feel you want to have or do or accomplish. But our message is that your universe is safe and abundant and always moving in a direction that allows you to manifest perfect scenarios and situations for your continued spiritual growth even though you're sometimes not able to perceive this is the case in certain situations. Perhaps this is one of those situations.

SHER: Well where's the spiritual growth in my suddenly having to worry about money when I never used to have to?

HS: And who has ordained that you should worry about money?

SHER: Me.

HS: Yes. Well, the money doesn't have anything to do with it. That's not part of the universal spiritual plan. The concern about money is coming from that part of you which is not your Divine Self, your God Self. That concern about money is a little game that can be treated like any other game. By that we mean you could decide to play or pass. We don't have a plan to present to you that would satisfy your financial desires. You don't have a plan that will satisfy your financial desires. No one out there is going to come to you with a plan to satisfy your financial desire, but when you are no longer concerned with your finances... your every need and desire will be accommodated.

SHER: Let go...and don't care...

HS: Caring is something that we do encourage, but latching on to a problem or difficultly that has no reality is not encouraged. It may seem very real to you, but we would remind you that you have created this thing that seems so very real and you have defined it as a lack or incompleteness or a challenge...something other than what you would call your ideal scenario.

It is put on your plate by your Higher Self to provide an opportunity for you to grow spiritually. What form might that growth take? In our opinion it comes in the form of realization. Self-realization. Perhaps realizing that the worries you have about financial matters or whatever agendas you have for the next step in your life are not as important as allowing what your Higher Self, with its Infinite and Divine wisdom, has already set in motion for your spiritual growth.

SHER: Sometimes I wonder if my declining client schedule is a sign I just need a break?

HS: It is designed to allow your Spirit to find that which satisfies, nurtures, and soothes it. Sometimes you need to be still and know. Sometimes you get too busy with "the work" as you perceive it to be and miss out on the opportunity, as Spirit perceives it, for your growth and good. So when things aren't following the agenda you have in mind, give Spirit an opportunity to do Its work. We guarantee beyond a shadow of a doubt that you will not be disappointed in the outcome.

SHER: Really? All I have to do is keep the faith? Sometimes that's very hard to do.

HS: We assure you that we would not deceive you in this truth. We love you and Truth and Love are synonymous. So it is our expression of unconditional love for you that leads us to remind you that Spirit has wonderful things in store for you. And you have been chugging along at great speed doing the good work, but it may be time to relax and allow.

You are an interesting dichotomy. You are so involved in the good work of Spirit introducing people to who they are and to their potential, yet sometimes you don't take the best care of yourself. We would remind you that you honor God when you honor yourself.

SHER: Can you tell me anything about my twin sister who has multiple sclerosis?

HS: Your sister is no less loved and supported than are any of God's creatures and even though her life experience is filled with challenge at this time it is also providing opportunity for tremendous spiritual growth. She is assisted by as many unseen forces on this side as she is assisted by you and other people in physicality. Her experience is of a beneficial nature for her and for all of you who come in contact with her in this lifetime.

SHER: What is she learning?

HS: She is learning that she is more than her body. She is learning that the way though pain is surrender. Surrender is the removal of resistance...the acceptance of God's love and the opportunity to serve other people in this lifetime. She is a gift to many, yourself included, who are interrelating through this challenging experience. All who relate in this situation are given the opportunity to experience love at depths far beyond what has ever been previously experienced. This is a great spiritual growth time for all of you in your relationship and identification with her.

SHER: Was there some kind of contract we had coming in that she'd be sick and I'd be the healer?

HS: Yes. You are aspects of the same essence. This may be difficult to comprehend because you are not focused on or aware of the grandeur of your beingness, the multi-dimensionality of yourselves. There are many ways that individuals are connected in a family way, a familiar way. Suffice it to say that you and your sister are part of the same soul group. There are others in that same soul group and there are many agreements between the numerous ones of you. The situation with your sister is particularly profound because of your agreement to be twins and to be identical and non-identical at the same time...identical with opposite life experiences during this limited focus in eternity that you call this incarnation.

We would wrap our loving arms around you, if we had them, to say that everything is going to be all right in eternity. That's not to say that your sister won't continue to deteriorate and die, but it is death simply of the physical body and the joyous shedding of that limitation and restriction...something you too will do someday. It will bring your soul back to join in blissful and delicious unification with the Oversoul that you both are.

SHER: If my sister had a choice, why would she make this choice?

HS: She was giving you an opportunity to understand sovereignty. She was giving you an opportunity to experience a situation where you can love someone, but you can't control someone. You can't step between them and the Divine blueprint of their life. You can't step between them and their creation. You are the creators the Creator created and each of you has the sovereign right to make choices and have the experiences those choices bring about. Even though your perspective may be limited—and you cannot fully appreciate the positive aspects of someone else's choice—that does not negate the absolute perfection of their life.

SHER: I've thought of moving to California, but worry about leaving other family members to care for my sister back home in Indiana.

HS: You have now jumped into future time and you are dealing with things beyond this Now Moment. And we understand your determination and desire to do the right thing. We remind you that there are powerful spiritual forces that are taking care of business, so to speak, so it's really not something you have to worry about.

We would again like to reassure you that you are loved and protected and guided and you are doing good work.

You are entitled to rest and not have to figure it all out. And you have every right to do it anyway you want so you may continue to stress over it if you want to, but we take this opportunity to remind you that you don't have to. There is no obligation for you to figure it all out. Don't worry about doing it right. You will do it right. You can't *not* do it right. And, you can do it effortlessly...without giving it a thought.

We offer you once again our unconditional love and remind you that the Voice of Spirit, the Holy Voice of Spirit, is as near to you as your heartbeat. And we would remind you that while it is perfectly acceptable for your own satisfaction or amusement to use other tools to gain this information—be it this channel or a psychic or whatever form you assign the ability to give voice to Spirit—we remind you that Spirit is always within you.

The Voice of Holy Spirit is your link to God, your creator, and it exists to assist you personally as much as it exists to help you help others. We remind you again, the key is to be still and know. And when invited, Spirit will speak. Our response is absolutely guaranteed one hundred percent of the time.

We leave you with our unconditional love and total devotion to your existence.

@@

Sher took a break from traveling and working so hard to rest and take care of family (her sister and her mom). A year after they both passed she met her twin soul (another healer) and is now living a whole new life knowing she is totally loved and supported both by Spirit and human beings in the physical world.

Lack of Creative Energy

"Allowing" was further explored during a session with our friend Gemma Grott, who came to "The We" during the sometimes frustrating process of writing her first book *God is in Hell: Opening My Heart to the Holocaust.*

GEMMA: I am feeling very compelled about my writing and sometimes it's a lot of fun and I feel like it's flowing and it's happening and other times I feel like it's not flowing at all and it's not fun and I become impatient, wanting results.

HS: We would also observe that another thing you spoke of today was your difficulty in understanding the concept of allowance. And so, our observation is...you will continue in this lifetime coming back to ongoing opportunities to have experiences that give you a chance to totally grasp the conceptual difference between "doing" and "being."

There possibly is a misunderstanding on your part that your sense of worth and accomplishment comes in doing... rather than fully appreciating the magnificence of simply being. It is the beingness of who you are that will further your spiritual growth, cultivating the ability to listen to the Voice of Spirit that communicates through your beingness and fulfills your destiny this incarnation. The thought that you must do something to fulfill a destiny is perhaps a misconception on your part. When you are creative and inspired and do your finest work it is an allowance of Spirit flowing through your open channel rather than self-generated energy, working to create a product that your mind has conceived. So when you are doing your best work on your book project, you are allowing Spirit to flow through you, and it is a great skill to enable this to occur for it takes some training and discipline to put ego aside because that aspect seems to think you have to work hard to produce whatever it is you feel will be your gift.

You have expressed, and we agree, that sometimes you feel inspired to work on your project and sometimes you don't and sometimes you feel guilty that you don't feel inspired and then you get in your own way. Or you feel like you should do such and such and it is not pleasurable. It is not satisfying. It is not even satisfactory work. So we would remind you that the opportunity that is in front of you is one of discernment to experience firsthand the difference between the product you produce when you feel you must be doing something, as opposed to the product you produce when you simply "be" and allow Spirit to flow through you. Is this of assistance to you?

GEMMA: Yes it is. I also recognize that this is a matter of not trusting and believing that Spirit will again inspire me during those long periods in between.

HS: It seems to us that the problem is not one of trusting Spirit to do that, but trusting the timing. You are not really believing that it will not happen. You are simply impatient with the timing in which it's happening. We would remind you that time is a construct of human physicality and is one of the many great illusions of physicality. There is no such thing as time and to allow an illusion to dominate your reality seems like a waste of time to us.

We would encourage you to drop your preconceptions of time and agendas and focus not on what will be accomplished in what amount of time, but to wait expectantly for the next magnificent creation to emerge from the great unknown into your consciousness with total disregard to the timing. We would suggest that nothing of a beneficial nature comes from putting forth a timetable agenda for what it is you wish to accomplish. On the one hand we would suggest you probably don't even know at this point what it is you're going to accomplish because it lives in the future and you cannot predict your future as a human. You can only come back to this present Now Moment and pay attention to what is in birth...in process of emerging. So rather than centering your energy and attention on what you must accomplish in some preconceived specific amount of time, watch the unfolding and birth and magnificence of what is waiting to spring forth—not from your doing, but from your being.

Are you comfortable with that?

GEMMA: Well, what am I supposed to "do" while I'm waiting? Do I do nothing or is there some preparation? My mind just keeps going to a "doing..."

HS: That is the point we are hoping to assist you with. Your whole essence keeps returning to the notion of having to "do" something. If you would like a homework assignment, your one and only assignment is to know that there is nothing to do. So, your hardest job is to stop doing your inclination to do.

GEMMA: Does that mean just staying calm and eating bon bons and reading novels?

HS: Or doing nothing. Bon bons and novels seem to

us to be another form of "doing." It seems to us that you are still making assignments. Perhaps more pleasurable assignments, and we have no quarrel with that, but we challenge you by asking, "What would it be like if you made no assignments? What would it be like if you wiped the slate clean...one hundred percent? What if you cleared the decks totally? What do you suppose you might discover if you were facing this void? What might be created from that absence of doingness?"

GEMMA: That's a good point. I have no idea. Imagine!

HS: Yes. We do recall a previous session that discussed the impatience on your part with meditation. And we return to that in loving assistance to you right now to suggest, that without putting a definition on what meditation may be, that you again consider the possibility that a meditative form of dismissing thought from your consciousness may be a launching pad for your next magnificent experience of manifesting your destiny and creating beyond your wildest dreams that which you desire to have authorship of.

GEMMA: Hmmm...so you're suggesting meditation?

HS: We are suggesting the process of "Be still and know." And that can come in whatever form you determine is appropriate for you. It does not have to be meditation as described or defined by any other person on the planet. It is simply an encouragement on our part for you to look at that part of yourself that you have as yet been unable to see, that would move you from your compulsive state of "doing" to the relaxed state of "being." You know where that is and what that is for you. We observe you are reluctant to look at it right now, for we sense a great fear on your part to stop "doing"—that perhaps your existence is threatened should you move to that mode of operation. We assure you that your existence is not threatened and your greatest achievement and completion and spiritual growth lies in that little dark corner of your being.

GEMMA: Thank you very much.

HS: How else may we be of assistance in this timing?

GEMMA: Well it's probably related to what you said about relaxing, but I feel my next step in growth has to do with connecting to my essential nature as a human... and I expect that that's connected with what we just talked about.

HS: We are sensitive at this timing to a misunderstanding on your part concerning "being" and "doing." We are sensing a confusion. Perhaps you may have a misconception that you cannot, for some reason, do things that you yearn to do or that call to you or that thrill you or hum for you and excite you. We wish to acknowledge that when you do those things that excite you the most, you are by one description "doing" rather than "being." But in the larger perspective you are "being" because you are fully being what it is that is the best expression of who you are. So don't confuse this conversation to think "being" means sitting and doing nothing. Being can also be doing. But it's doing something effortlessly with the core of your being in absolute ecstasy and it doesn't have any "chore nature" to it. It doesn't have any difficulty to it and it doesn't have any effort to it because it is the out-flowing expression of your true nature and desire.

So we would, as an example, point to your dancing in the streets—that joyous, effortless, blissful, love-filled experience being a perfect example of your "being" as opposed to "doing," even though you were doing something. The doing aspect is overtaken by the expression of your being.

Now if you can draw the equation between that and the producing of your book, to understand that when you're doing the book you are doing something. But it's an expression from deep within your being, rather than sitting down and feeling like you should be thinking out chapters or paragraphs or sentences.

The book comes in the same manner that the joy of dancing does...and that was an allowance. That was giving yourself permission to just flow in the joy of the experience from the depth of your being.

We just revel in the magnificence of who you are as human beings. We have very tender, compassionate thoughts about your self-imposed struggle. We see the process you create to experience your inadequacies because that is the only way you can then experience overcoming your inadequacies. And so we are in the midst of seeing where you are...and seeing who you are...and seeing the potential of the thrill of your own discovery of who you are. And we see that it's not always an easy journey for you because unfortunately you do not have the greater perspective to see yourselves as we see you in all your magnificence.

And so, we invite you now to let all thought leave your mind and rest here in the silence of the moment to just be. Simply experience the quietness and the stillness now of your own consciousness.

☺☺

Gemma is currently living the life of her dreams in a state of ecstasy in Hawaii. She has built a lovely home. Her mortgage is paid and the universe provides her abundance. She has established herself in a community of friends where she follows Spirit from moment to moment and does as she is prompted. Some days she writes, some days she dances. Everyday she communes with nature and spends extraordinary amounts of time just "being" with the ocean.

Procrastination

"The We" helped us understand that the nature of our personal reality is totally up to us. We get to choose whether we'll see the glass as half empty or half full. Since we're creating our personal reality through our beliefs, thoughts, and feelings, everything we experience has the potential to be seen through a positive perspective. We've learned that the alternative to the common human tendency to see things through the eyes of fear is to shift perspective and view everything through the eyes of love. Shifting to the new perspective is finding the blessing in an experience and using it to grow. It's surrendering our victimization and reclaiming our power as co-creators. "The We" have continually challenged us to find more opportunities to shift from a negative to a positive perspective.

JIM: I have a question. When one runs into habitual patterns, for example procrastination (which has been a pattern in my life) what do you recommend or what exercises or realizations do you offer?

HS: It might be helpful when you recognize that you have procrastinated, to explore what the hidden significance of that procrastination is. You may find a very valid reason for not taking on or completing a project. You may be very justified in putting a project aside because your Higher Self has something in mind that will be more significant to your learning or to enriching your life. If you could think of a situation where you procrastinated and see what occurred while you were not doing what you thought you should and see what that provided in your life, it might be quite an eye-opener. And we're saying not to judge the experience by what did or didn't physically get accomplished, but take a look at the other dynamics that were active and what they provided in the way of your own self discovery.

Did a specific procrastination come to mind?

JIM: Yes. I became ill at the end of school. I managed to get grades out, but I haven't gotten my write-ups out and I feel like I've been procrastinating on that for a while now. I've recovered my health, but I haven't completed my project.

HS: And can you put your attention now on what you did accomplish while the grades waited patiently for your attention?

JIM: Yes.

HS: And how do you feel about what you did accomplish?

JIM: I feel good. I accomplished a lot.

HS: So maybe you're not a procrastinator. Maybe you're an "allower." Maybe you're allowing your universe to unfold whether or not you can see the purpose of your direction. We suggest you look back now over the road you've traveled and you will most likely recognize the beneficial rewards of your actions—even though you may have judged yourself "not on course" with what you thought you should be doing. There are no accidents. There are no points of your life that aren't purposeful. There are no events that are wrong or insignificant. They all have meaning. Your challenge—your mission, should you choose to accept it—is to recognize the richness of each experience, each relationship, each problem.

IX

Conclusion

On a sunny afternoon in June of 2004, a group of women gathered in the shade of our backyard deck in Alamo to once again enjoy each other's company, conversation, and refreshments. It was a time of joyous reconnection after a long absence from their group get-togethers and it was seen as an opportunity for spiritual as well as emotional reconnection.

That afternoon's transmission was a perfect summary of the primary message we had been receiving from "The We" for three decades and it reiterated nicely the teaching that has been offered throughout this book. I believe these principles are so crucial to our inner sense of well-being and overall happiness and harmony that they cannot be overstated. I wish to thank these women for bravely asking their questions on behalf of all of us who struggle with our own similar fears and doubts.

Reiterating the Basics

QUESTIONER: I don't know what to ask, but I'm feeling fear and anxiety and depression.

HS: We would suggest that our method of being of service is to remind you who you are. As you deal moment-to-moment, hour-to-hour and day-to-day with what you judge to be problems, you have usually forgotten who you are. So perhaps you would like to begin by sharing a concern or an issue or question of a personal nature that we might be able to assist you in sorting through to view from a higher perspective that may ease the burden and allow you to more fully appreciate that which is occurring in your life. Does this make sense to you?

GROUP: Yes.

HS: So then, who would like to be first?

QUESTIONER: I have been full of fear over finances because I have not been able to work. I've had anxiety attacks, panic attacks, depression and I don't know what that's all about. I've been working forever and now for me to even think about work I get sick to my stomach. And yet, I need to make money.

HS: We understand. And we would remind you first of all, although when you're anxious or when you're fearful this is the last thing that seems to be true, but we are here to remind you that it is true and it is the basic essence of who you are: you are not a victim and you are always the creator of your reality, the creator of your experience. And sometimes when it seems as if life is dealing you a bad hand, it's because you have forgotten who you are. You have forgotten that you are "the creator that God created you to be." You are allowing your fears and doubts to manifest, rather than the more desirable, positive elements that you also have the capability of manifesting. It is important to first realize that life does not come "at you." Life comes "through you." When you are frightened or anxious or depressed these feelings that seem by objective reasoning to be negative are actually gifts. They are messengers that are waking you up and giving you an opportunity to make new choices. It can be new choices in how you see your experience. It can be new choices of what you believe to be true in your life. And if you will examine beliefs to determine whether or not they continue to serve you, when you find one that no longer serves you in the manner you desire and change that belief, we guarantee you will have a new experience.

Can you give some thought at this point to the nature of the "fear thoughts" and perhaps, if you wish, you could share with us that which frightens you right now concerning your work life.

QUESTIONER: One is that I need to get out and work. I'm angry with myself because I haven't taken care of myself financially. I see myself at the age of 61 and I haven't done those things. And another piece of it is that it scares me because I'm not sure what my capabilities are anymore. I absolutely freeze up when I start trying to do work. My mind freezes up. I think if I can get motivated and moving the rest is going to come.

HS: We would absolutely agree and support that line of thinking—that life from moment to moment is choice and the choice regardless of what it appears to be always comes down to one of two things. You will choose to function and think from fear or you will choose to function and think and act from love. When your egoic mind starts to prattle on with thoughts of doubt about your ability, or doubt about money—particularly doubt about the abundance of the universe to provide what you need when you need it—when these voices of fear come up and you choose to align with them, anxiety or fear or depression are the ultimate result, the only result that can come from having made the choice to believe that is the truth. When you choose from love, which recognizes your abundance right here, right now in this moment—recognizes your safety right here, right now, in this moment, breathing in air, breathing in life, sending out love and having connections in warm and loving relationships—when you experience your life from that Love Perspective, all is well.

But that gets defeated when you jump into the future and wonder what's going to happen next week or next month or tomorrow. But it's just a game. It's just a story. And the truth of the matter is, you're not your game or your story. You're not even your body or your role. The truth is you are an infinite, everlasting spirit who right here, right now has chosen to be physical, to be in a human body and play all the scenarios that some higher aspect of yourself creates. The question is: are you going to allow your creator to be your ego or your Spirit? There are always those two choices within that one mind that you are. Is this of value to you?

QUESTIONER: Yes.

HS: Thank you.

NEW QUESTIONER: I would like to ask about plans for moving from my old job to my new job and also about my son. Is this a positive move?

HS: Please understand we are here to assist you in

anyway we can with absolute love, however we are not the creators of your universe. You are the creator of your universe, so we can't answer what is the best thing, or what is the right thing. There is no best or right or wrong.

Your best counsel from us, with love, is "be still and know." And by that we mean center yourself, calm yourself at any given moment in time when an important decision is to be made. For as we said before, "Life is merely choices at any given moment." And the choice is always, no matter how complicated your story line makes it appear to be—the choice is always so simple—it's the choice for fear or the choice for love.

Those are the two powers of the universe. We will assure you that the choice for love is so much more powerful that fear doesn't stand a chance when love is placed in its presence. So our best loving guidance for you is "be still and know." Stop the world. Go into your heart. Ask for guidance as to what is the loving decision in the matter—whether it be with your friends, your son, your mate, your boss. No one outside of yourself knows the answer to the question better than you in the heart of your being. You have a Higher Consciousness, higher than your ego consciousness, that is guiding you every step of the way through this life. Is that of help?

QUESTIONER: Yes. I know in my heart it's the right thing and I'm doing this with a good heart, and so it's going to be right for my son.

HS: Fear and doubt are mankind's greatest enemies. And fear and doubt both come from the ego mind.

Mind has two parts. The part of the mind through which we function allows for the expression of Spirit and there is always room for that in every mind, in the One mind. And we understand that we share that mind with ego. Ego does not understand that it shares that mind with Spirit. But we understand that we share that mind with ego and we would just remind you that among the many choices that you make is always the choice between Spirit-mind thoughts and ego-mind thoughts. You get to choose.

We would also like to suggest you give some thought to the Trinity. The Trinity is the Father, the Son, and the Holy Ghost. The news is: you are the Trinity. You are the Father, the Son and the Holy Ghost. Some would think that blasphemy, but this Holy Voice of Spirit assures you that you are an expression of Divinity. That connection with God/Father is you. You are also God's Son. That Holy expression of Divinity is you. We are Holy Spirit. That Holy expression of Divinity is also within you. Although we are speaking through this body at this moment, we are speaking from the same Oneness that is within you.

NEW QUESTIONER: Do you have a message for me?

HS: (Pause.) You are loved more than you'll ever know. You are never alone for We are here. We have always been here. We always will be here. We're here to assist you and we never impose our will on you. If you would like our assistance, all you have to do is ask. We come by invitation and nothing can bar our relationship with you in the generation of love and truth and beauty.

When you think you have problems take this reminder that problems are merely messengers. They remind you of those areas in your life where faith is lacking. When you can stop and freeze frame in the midst of your problems and see that all that has really happened is that faith is missing right here, right now, and when you restore that faith and know that you are not alone, you have the power of the Almighty supporting you—problems will solve themselves. And the reason that problems will solve themselves is because they have no further need to exist. They only existed in the first place as messengers to "wake you up."

Blessings to you.

NEW QUESTIONER: I'm having a hard time clarifying my question. I'd like to do something different with my life. I'm having a hard time seeking out...

HS: Are you stuck?

QUESTIONER: Yes.

HS: We would remind you that you are not stuck. We understand you feel like you're stuck, but you're just creating the same thing over again.

Again, we would advise you to "be still and know" and in the calmness of stilling the ego-mind and allowing Spirit to speak through your heart and mind it will become very clear what makes your heart sing and what you desire and what direction you need to pursue. And then we would encourage you to be bold, be brave. Take the step that breaks the cycle that keeps you recreating the same thing you created prior to this that makes you feel like you're stuck. We absolutely guarantee you that you are not stuck. You are never not the creator of your reality. Your thoughts and beliefs in this moment are like building blocks or blueprints that will determine the manifestation of the next Now Moment that you experience as your life. So take this opportunity to take a bigger look at your life. No matter how much it feels like you're in a rut or a routine, you are not stuck. Does this make sense to you?

QUESTIONER: (Quiet.)

HS: Are you happy with this?

(Laughter.)

Many people aren't.

(Pause.)

You'll get over it. And when you do there awaits such joy and bliss and excitement for you to know that you truly do control your destiny every step of the way. And you are not a victim and you can have it any way that you want it. The way it is right now is a direct result of your vibratory frequency and your energy and your thought processes and your belief systems. None of this has happened by accident. And this is not a lecture that has a judgment. This is a statement of spiritual physics. It is just simply, whether science or the world recognizes it or not, the way the universe works. And, it's not a problem...it's a joy.

We feel that this is sufficient to the time. We thank you for your bold and brave willingness to explore who you are. Some of the reflections we have held up to you may have startled or irritated you, but we know that your spiritual growth has been enhanced by this.

We wish you our unconditional love and we remind you that our loving support is available to you anytime, anyplace. We speak through this body in this chair at this time, but we exist on dimensions that are so much grander and we are available to each and every one of you.

Finding Your Voice Within

Our purpose in sharing our experience with "The We" is two-fold. Denny and I decided to publish this channeled material because we, and so many people who have been exposed to it, find this New Perspective helpful when applied to our daily lives. Simply said, the material rings true in our hearts and putting the material into practice has made a real difference in our lives. We hope that by sharing our experience with you we can inspire you to a life in which Spirit comes first. The other reason for publishing this book is to encourage you to find your own Inner Voice.

Since I was thirteen and first started in radio, my job has been to be a messenger, bringing people news of a world reality "out there." Now, in this new relationship with "The We," I feel like a new kind of messenger, bringing people news of a reality "in here." The New Perspective takes a look underneath physical reality at the level where it is created.

Perhaps one of the most important messages received from "The We" is that life is a metaphor. Our lives are reflections of our inner reality. Everything on the invisible inner level, such as our beliefs about reality and our feelings about what we believe, is manifested in the outer physical world to help us work through experiences for the growth and development of the soul. It is our hope in sharing these dialogues that we have given you the motivation to examine your own beliefs, to question your viewpoints, to push the envelope and look at the symbols manifesting in your life.

The other thing the last twenty years of channeling has taught us is that there is unquestionably a wise and magnificent teacher living within each and every one of you. When invited to speak, that Voice of Spirit is easily accessible and incredibly helpful.

Your communication with this wise and loving source may not take the form ours did. It has been our experience that Spirit speaks in many ways.

When I originally began channeling, I made contact with Spirit in a trance state. Since then my relationship to the Voice of Spirit has become much more casual and informal. I am now able to know at a very deep level when thoughts passing through my mind represent the loving Voice of Spirit, as opposed to when they are simply the fear-based thoughts of my ego.

Denny's relationship with the Voice of Spirit is the heart of her practice as a Marriage and Family Therapist. She never enters the sanctity of her office for a therapeutic session with a client without first inviting Spirit to be present, guiding everything she says and does for the higher good of all concerned.

We have both learned to trust and respect the guidance that flows through us during these sacred times. This rich experience is available to all of you and we encourage you to make contact in whatever manner is comfortable for you. With a little bit of practice you can free yourself from the chatter of the ego long enough for this higher wisdom to come through.

Guided hypnotherapy journeys can be another effective way of making contact with the Voice of Spirit. A skilled hypnotherapist can facilitate a personal and profound question and answer session between you and your Human Subconscious, Higher Self, or Holy Spirit. The entire dialogue will take place using your spirit ears and imagination, within the privacy of your mind. Whether you share the messages you receive with your hypnotherapist or others is totally up to you. You can have an inspired experience with the help of a good facilitator.

Marriage and Family Therapist Holly Holmes-Meredith trains hypnotherapists at H.C.H Institute for Hypnotherapy and Psycho-Spiritual Trainings in Lafayette, California. She has facilitated more than twenty thousand hypnotherapy sessions and knows their profound and lasting effects. Holly says, "By invoking the client's Higher Self, clients are able to access expanded states of consciousness similar to those experienced in meditation or in profound states of presence—states where the egoic or self-involved consciousness is transcended or simply out of the way. Through these transpersonal states of consciousness healing and profound change can take place effortlessly."

"The Higher Self," says Holly, "is an aspect of human consciousness that goes beyond our waking, ordinary consciousness and can access certain wisdom not experienced in normal consciousness." More information on the Higher Self experience available through hypnotherapy can be found at www.hypnotherapytraining.com.

As appreciative students of *A Course in Miracles*, we take to heart the promises made regarding listening to "The Teacher within." Our experience with "The We" has demonstrated to our satisfaction the enriching role Holy Spirit can play when welcomed into our lives.

On page 52 of *A Course in Miracles* in the *Manual for Teachers* it is written:

"The teacher of God must...learn to use words in a new way. Gradually, he learns how to let his words be chosen for him by ceasing to decide for himself what he will say. This process is merely a special case of the lesson in the workbook that says, 'I will step back and let Him lead the way.' The teacher of God accepts the words that are offered him, and gives as he receives. He does not control the direction of his speaking. He listens and hears and speaks."

The *Manual for Teachers* goes on to say on page 59:

"The limits the world places on communication are the chief barriers to direct experience of the Holy Spirit, Whose Presence is always there and Whose Voice is available but for the hearing."

We have both come to rely more and more on that Voice Within in our daily lives. Or perhaps we should say we put Spirit in charge more and more when we remember to stay conscious enough to recognize that we are Divine Sons of God and always connected to His Spirit. We are inspired and expanded in our awareness by these practical words from page 68 of the *Manual for Teachers*:

"To ask the Holy Spirit to decide for you is simply to accept your true inheritance. Does this mean that you cannot say anything without consulting Him? No, indeed! That would hardly be practical, and it is the practical with which this course is most concerned. If you have made it a habit to ask for help when and where you can, you can be confident that wisdom will be given you when you need it. Prepare for this each morning, remember God when you can throughout the day, ask the Holy Spirit's help when it is feasible to do so, and thank Him for His guidance at night. And your confidence will be well founded indeed.

Never forget that the Holy Spirit does not depend on your words. He understands the requests of your heart, and answers them."

To which, from our personal experience, we say, "Amen."

When Denny and I take these insights from *A Course in Miracles* and combine them with our personal experience with "The We," we arrive at an eye-opening understanding of the Holy Trinity. When, as children in Sunday school, we first heard about the Father, Son and Holy Ghost, it was a fascinating parable, but a concept that we just didn't "get." In our child minds it was much easier to understand the concept of conscience or an Inner Voice as portrayed by Jiminy Cricket in Walt Disney's *Pinocchio* movie than it was to grasp the idea of a Holy Spirit—let alone a Voice for God. We were both taught as children to honor the voice of conscience within and we were told it would always guide us down the proper path during all of life's decision-making processes. For most of our lives we have honored and respected that Voice Within, so it's not a new concept for us.

However, our experience with "The We," coupled with the words concerning Holy Spirit that are found in *A Course in Miracles*, opens the door to a greater understanding of the Trinity and where we fit in the trilogy.

Here's a reminder of what "The We" told us about the Holy Trinity:

"Our way of being of service is to act as the third aspect of the Trinity. So those of you who are familiar with the

Father, the Son, and the Holy Ghost know who the Father is and know who the Son is. You, male and female, are the Son."

"The We" go on to say: "We are the Holy Ghost. We are the Spirit. We are the connection. We are the link between you and your Father. We are the bridge between you and your Creator. We are the link that will help you complete your destiny. We are always available."

Now, having been exposed to both quantum physics and the words of "The We," it dawns on us that the Father is the Wave. The Son is both wave and particle. We remember learning that at the sub-atomic level matter is both wave and particle, solidifying as it is observed. It then becomes clear to us that the Father or God is a non-physical consciousness. Since we are created in His image, we too are consciousness, despite having created a physical body. We are, however, more than that body. We are Spirit wearing a human disguise. Our eternal nature is the Wave and exists forever. Our physical nature is the particle and only exists from physical birth to death.

The third part of The Trinity is Holy Spirit—the connection between the Wave (God) and the particle (man)—the link between us and our Creator, the connection between body and Spirit, the seen and the unseen. The Voice of Spirit reminds us that we are both human and Divine, matter and Spirit, particle and Wave.

You are never alone. You have never been alone. You will never be alone. The link to God, the Voice for God, is always with you, always within you. It completes the Holy Trinity: the Father, the Son and the Holy Spirit.

How to Connect with Your Inner Voice

In our experience, the secret to receiving the gifts of Spirit once you have invited Its presence is to observe your thoughts rather than to create your thoughts. It's a matter of hearing, seeing, or feeling the inspired words, recognizing them and then repeating them. It's important not to judge them as they're coming through.

Once they've manifested you can evaluate them. If there's any form of fear or judgment attached to the message, we suggest the message has been corrupted by your personality self and came from your ego and not from Spirit. Spirit always extends and communicates love, whereas the ego projects fear in one form or another.

Preparations: First decide if you would prefer this to be a solo experience or if you're comfortable having a companion. Find a quiet spot where you won't be disturbed for at least half an hour. Be sure to turn off the phone. You might even put a "Do not disturb" sign on your door.

You need a tape recorder to record your experience. You will be speaking out loud the messages you receive. If you decide to have a friend accompany you, he or she can take notes if you don't have a tape recorder. Your companion can ask the questions you're wanting answered so you can remain in the passive role of channeling Spirit. Either way you will want a record of what comes forth.

If you're doing this solo, limit yourself to one question. Decide in advance what question you want to ask. Be sure to write down your question because once you've connected with Spirit you don't want to break that connection by trying to remember what to ask.

Step One: Sit in a comfortable position. Close your eyes.

Step Two: Begin a process of deep relaxation. Imagine that a wave of energy is moving through your body from the top of your head to the tip of your toes. As this energy moves through you it opens and relaxes every cell of your body. As this relaxation occurs, focus on your breathing. Pay attention to the gentle flow of your breath—moving in and moving out.

Step Three: As you relax and quiet your mind, ask in a very deep way for Spirit to come forth and speak through you for the highest good of all concerned. If you're doing this alone, now is the time to ask Spirit to speak through you and answer your question. If you are working with a partner, ask Spirit to speak through you for your higher good and the higher good of all concerned...and then allow your partner to present any number of questions.

Step Four: Listen with your Spirit ears to whatever comes to you. Observe the words that pass through your awareness and speak them out loud. You may feel that this is just your imagination. Don't let that distract you. Continue to speak whatever words come to you. Allow it to flow.

Step Five: When the process is complete return to your ordinary state of consciousness. It may take a few minutes to "tune back in" to your surroundings. Take a moment to feel gratitude for the words you have received. It is at this point that your experience will begin to fade, much like a dream fades from memory upon awakening. You'll be very happy that the words have been captured and saved. Now listen to the recorded answers to your questions.

The Voice for God lives within each of us. Accessing that Voice puts you in direct contact with Spirit. Using this process, there is no need for a middleman to facilitate your communion with your Creator. Denny and I wish you ever-expanding awareness, growing consciousness, unlimited abundance and magnificent spiritual growth.

Namaste.

X

Acknowledgments

The book cover is a co-creation of photographer Kimall Christensen and artist Trea Christopher Grey. Visit their online gallery of delights at www.worldsofgoodfortune.com.

Special thanks to our loyal editor Leda Ciraolo, Ph.D., whose guidance and organizational skills have been invaluable. She can be reached at *The Written Word®*, Oakland, California, or by email at: ledaciraolo@sbcglobal.net.

We have special appreciation for our friend David Cates, who helped point us in the right direction, bringing a larger perspective to our work.

We also wish to acknowledge our friends of the heart and companions of the soul for their support and encouragement of our work. Thanks to Dr. Sharon Wesch, Jim and Faye McCaughan, Gemma Grott, Glenda Hesseltine, Paul Meredith and Holly Holmes Meredith. Special appreciation is given to all the others who participated with open minds in "The We" dialogues over the years.

About the Authors

Since 1989 Denny has been a Marriage and Family Therapist, licensed by the state of California and practicing in Lafayette, California. Denny has been a spiritual seeker since early childhood. Her inquiring mind earned her a college scholarship in debate at College of the Pacific in Stockton, California, where she met and married Ron. For twenty years Denny was a housewife and mother, raising two sons. When they left the nest in the 1980's she pursued her dream of becoming a Marriage and Family Therapist. In the ensuing years she has passionately combined psychotherapy with Spiritual Consciousness, encouraging all who come to her to explore their deeper connection to Spirit. Denny can be reached at: dennyreynolds@aol.com.

Ron retired from radio broadcasting in 2004 after fifty years in radio and television. He now devotes his time to spiritual studies, writing, and teaching workshops that assist others in their own Self-Realization. He continues to channel "The We" and is available by special arrangement for private sessions with HS. Ron can be reached at ronjreynolds@aol.com.

Together, Ron and Denny have co-founded and direct

165

The New Perspective, a Spiritual Foundation. Their website is www.thenewperspective.com. They can be reached at P.O. Box 695, Alamo, CA 94507 or at (925) 552-0576.

Other Books in *The New Perspective Trilogy*
by Ron and Denny Reynolds

The New Perspective: Ten Tools for Self-Transformation, published July 2005 and available from Trafford Publishing. Order on-line at www.trafford.com/04-2593.html.

Art of Relationship: The New Perspective, published July 2006 and available from Trafford Publishing. Order on-line at www.trafford.com/06-0073.html.

You may also contact:
Trafford Publishing
Suite 6E, 2333 Government Street
Victoria, B.C., Canada V8T4P4
Phone 250-383-6864
Toll free 1-888-232-4444 (Canada and U.S. only).

ISBN 142511554-3